Torta *della* Nonna

Torta *della* Nonna

A collection of the best homemade Italian desserts

Emiko Davies

Hardie Grant

BOOKS

Introduction

Making sweets was my first foray into cooking independently in the kitchen, and as a teenager I could often be found baking my way through my mother's cookbooks, in particular an American pie cookbook – I have always had a thing for pastry. You will see a bias towards it in this book too, from southern Italian custard and jam *bocconotti* to ricotta-filled crostata and Florence's little rice pudding pastries, *budini di riso*.

I also have a thing for historic Italian cookbooks, as they have been instrumental in helping me appreciate the unchanging nature of regional Italian cuisine, as well as being a constant source of inspiration for recipes. They are as close as you can get to unlocking the recipes of nonna. My Tuscan mother-in-law, in fact, relied on her mother for recipes, who, in turn, like so many Italian housewives of her generation, relied on her Artusi.

A thick copy of Pellegrino Artusi's 1891 cookbook, *Science in the Kitchen and the Art of Eating Well*, with its 790 recipes, was often given to Italian brides to guide them in the kitchen. My mother-in-law's copy (inherited from her mother) is so well-worn that the spine is broken and the book automatically opens to Artusi's three recipes for *pasta frolla* (Italy's soft shortcrust pastry) and there is a little mark next to recipe B – my preferred of the three, too, and one of the essentials in my kitchen today.

In fact, many of the recipes in this book have their beginnings in that very *pasta frolla*. Many are the kind of recipes that Carol Field refers to in her excellent *The Italian Baker* (1985), sweets that 'have perfumed mountain homes in Val d'Aosta, simple farmhouses near Bologna, villas in the Tuscan countryside, and apartments in Rome. Emanating from a simple way of life, they almost invariably start with *pasta frolla*.'

A few decades after Artusi's publication, in 1929, a Roman magazine editor, Ada Boni, published *Il Talismano della Felicità* (*The Talisman of Happiness*, an enormous collection of more than 1000 classic recipes) and, along with Artusi, it became the *Joy of Cooking* for many Italian households too. Her book is still an important reference book, the recipes still very much valid today, like Artusi's, but easier to follow for a modern reader in a modern kitchen than Artusi's charming, nineteenth-century banter-filled recipes. From granita to stuffed peaches and the wonderful thrifty chocolate cake (a dense cake made with only pantry items and milk, no eggs or butter), Boni's no-nonsense recipes are still among some of my favourites when I want to produce something that channels my inner nonna.

These recipes, which first appeared in my cookbooks, *Florentine*, *Acquacotta* and *Tortellini at Midnight*, along with a handful of new inclusions, are a collection of beloved Italian classics, many of which you could likely find on nonna's table for Sunday lunch, in a homely trattoria or one of Florence's best pastry shops.

Cook's notes

Cooking times and temperatures

Recipes were tested on a standard gas stovetop. You may need to adjust the heat or cooking times slightly for induction or electric stovetops.

Baking recipes were all baked in a standard conventional oven with an oven thermometer. If you are using a fan-forced or convection oven, you may need to decrease the temperature by 20°C (35°F) or adjust the cooking time.

Measurements

I always measure recipe ingredients by metric weight. It is the way Italians cook and it is the most reliable way to measure out ingredients in a recipe. I suggest doing the same for best results, particularly for baked goods.

This book uses 20 ml (¾ fl oz) tablespoons; if you are working with 15 ml (½ fl oz) tablespoons, be generous with your tablespoon measurements.

Metric cup measurements are used, i.e. 250 ml (8½ fl oz) for 1 cup; in the US, 1 cup is 237 ml (8 fl oz), so American cooks should be generous with their cup measurements; in the UK, 1 cup is 284 ml (9½ fl oz), so British cooks should be scant with their cup measurements.

Eggs

Where possible, use free-range, organic eggs that are approximately 55 g (2 oz), which corresponds to 'large' eggs in the US, Canada and Australia, and 'medium' eggs in Europe. It is ideal to bake with room temperature eggs, especially if you need their lift when whipped, but if you have forgotten to leave them out of the fridge at least 30 minutes before using, you can warm them up gently but quickly by putting them in a bowl of very warm water for 5 minutes.

Butter

In Italy, it is most common to use unsalted butter in baking, so this is why unsalted butter is called for in these recipes. If using salted butter, do take into account that the flavour will change slightly.

Recipes for pastry will require very cold butter. This is very important, especially if you're working in a warm kitchen, such as in the summer. Some cake recipes will require room temperature butter. If you have forgotten to leave the butter out for at least 30 minutes to soften before using (I usually dice it to help it along), a quick solution is to grate the cold butter with a cheese grater and leave it spread out on a tray for 5 minutes before using.

Sugar

Sugar is white granulated sugar unless otherwise specified.

Flour

Most Italian cake and biscuit recipes call for white, soft wheat flour, which is usually labelled *Tipo 00* in Italian. This number refers to how refined the flour is. In other countries, it can be replaced with white, all-purpose flour. You may find other flours make a stiffer batter and require additional liquid.

Alchermes

Alchermes is a scarlet-tinged alcohol that dates back to the Renaissance and is almost exclusively used for staining desserts the same vivid pink colour, such as in the *Corolli rossi* (page 101), *Zuccotto* (page 141), *Tronco al cioccolato* (page 117) and *Zuppa inglese* (page 146). The best version is one that you can find in the pharmacy of Florence's Santa Maria Novella church; it's a recipe that they've been using since 1743. Once known as the

liquore dei Medici, it was touted as a long-life elixir, used to cure palpitations of the heart and measles, and to revive 'weary spirits'. Flavoured with spices such as cinnamon, vanilla, cloves and nutmeg, it also has a strong balsamic and medicinal character. It is turned scarlet by a natural red dye, made from the infusion of dried insects, *kermes* (hence the name) or cochineal. Some may be put off by the thought of this, but you have probably already come across it as 'natural food dye' and it is a much better option than the synthetic version of red dye, which is a known carcinogen and banned in some countries, including the United States and Norway.

If you don't have Alchermes, you can sometimes find a similar pink syrup especially for dessert preparations called *bagno per i dolci*. Otherwise you can use another liqueur such as rum, kirsch, Grand Marnier, or even vin santo or another dessert wine. Where you are using the Alchermes to soak biscuits or sponge, you can also use a simple syrup and skip the alcohol.

Chilling pastry

If you're trying to roll out pastry in the hot, sweltering summer and find that it's melting before your eyes, try placing a couple of bags of frozen peas (or similar, even ice packs) directly onto the surface where you plan to roll the pastry out for about 10 minutes to chill it. Always chill your pastry before using it (letting it rest in the fridge for 1 hour is ideal). You might even go so far as to put the rolling pin in the freezer to give it some chill. The idea is to keep the pastry (and the butter in it) cold so that you can work with it more easily.

Yeast and rising dough

In Italy, fresh yeast is readily available at supermarkets and is more commonly used than dried yeast. As a very simple rule, the less yeast used, the longer the dough will need to rise (overnight, for example, in the fridge) and you will be rewarded with a better-developed flavour, better texture and longer-lasting bread. But if you are in a hurry and you only want to let the bread rise for 1 hour (at a minimum), keep it in a warm place to encourage it to rise more quickly. If it's winter and your kitchen is cold, you can even warm up the oven a little, turn it off, then put the bowl in the warmed oven.

Blind baking

Blind baking helps to ensure that the bottom crust of a tart cooks through properly in certain recipes, such as the *Torta della nonna* (page 61) and the *Torta di semolino e cioccolato* (page 119). Press the pastry into the pie dish and cover with a sheet of baking paper. Fill with baking beads (you can also use dried beans or uncooked rice – you can keep these 'baking beans' in a jar and re-use specifically for this purpose). Bake in the oven as per the recipe, then remove the paper and beads and continue with the recipe.

Gelato-making

The gelato recipes in this book work best with an ice-cream machine. Home-made gelato usually benefits from a rest in the freezer for at least an hour before serving. If it has been in the freezer overnight or longer, remove the gelato about 15 minutes before serving.

Bain-marie (double boiler)

A bain-marie ensures gentle cooking for things such as melting chocolate or the sponge batter for *Savoiardi* (page 17), which helps to keep the airy batter stable. To prepare a bain-marie, set a heatproof bowl over a saucepan with about 2.5 cm (1 in) simmering water. Make sure the bowl is not touching the water.

Cook's notes

Crema pasticcera Pastry cream/ *Savoiardi*/ *Torta al cioccolato* Chocolate cake/ *Crostata di marmellata* Apricot jam tart/ *Torta margherita* Margherita sponge cake

Essenziali/

Essentials

Recipes to master, from *crema*, the sweet custard cream that fills pastries, tarts and puddings alike, to the perfect *pasta frolla*, a sweet shortcrust pastry inspired by a nineteenth-century recipe.

Crema pasticcera

PASTRY CREAM

This is a simple, traditional preparation for pastry cream, a thick Italian custard, which is used to fill pastries such as *Bomboloncini* (page 48), *Cornetti* (page 38) and *Sfogliatine* (page 44) and to fill cakes such as *Schiacciata alla Fiorentina* (page 108) and the *Torta della nonna* (page 61). Depending on what you are using this pastry cream for, you may like to add some subtle flavour with lemon zest or vanilla. This recipe can easily be halved if you don't need the amount that it makes here.

Makes about 680 g (1½ lb) of pastry cream

4 egg yolks
120 g (4½ oz) sugar
30 g (1 oz) cornflour (cornstarch)
500 ml (17 fl oz/2 cups) warm milk
zest of 1 lemon or 1 teaspoon natural vanilla extract or ½ vanilla bean (optional), split lengthways and seeds scraped

Whisk the egg yolks and sugar together in a mixing bowl until pale. Stir in the cornflour. Put the mixture in a saucepan over a low heat and add the warm milk, little by little, stirring between each addition. Add the lemon zest or vanilla extract or seeds, if using. Stir continuously with a whisk or a wooden spoon until the mixture becomes smooth and thick, about 10 minutes. You are looking for a consistency similar to mayonnaise (when cool, it will also firm up further). Do not let it boil – remove from the heat at the very first sign of a bubble.

Remove the pastry cream from the heat. Prepare an ice bath and cool the pastry cream quickly by transferring to a mixing bowl set over the ice water. Cover with plastic wrap, making sure that the plastic is touching the surface of the pastry cream so it doesn't develop a skin. Keep in the fridge until needed.

Savoiardi

Also known as 'lady fingers', savoiardi are widely used in Italian desserts, namely for soaking up liqueur or coffee and layering into a dish with *crema* for a trifle-like *Zuppa inglese* (page 146) or tiramisu. They're also great simply as a mid-morning treat dipped into coffee.

Savoiardi are nothing more than *pan di spagna* (Italian sponge cake) dried out in the oven so they last a long time in the pantry. They are a conveniently small size, which makes layering into glasses or a wide dish for other desserts very handy. Named for the House of Savoy, the last monarchs of Italy, they are especially tied to the regions where the Savoys had significant history: Sicily, Sardinia and Piedmont.

They're relatively easy to make and so quick to bake, but a piping bag does help to get the right shape. Otherwise you can try making them like a drop biscuit (as simple as dropping blobs of batter off a spoon) for round ones, which are still perfectly suited for dipping into coffee or custard and are arguably more convenient if you are making individual cups of *zuppa inglese*.

Makes 24 biscuits

120 g (4½ oz) sugar
3 eggs
120 g (4½ oz) plain (all-purpose)
    flour, sifted
50 g (1¾ oz) icing (confectioners')
    sugar (optional)

Preheat the oven to 200°C (400°F).

In a metal bowl set over a bain-marie (double boiler; see page 10) of simmering water, beat the sugar and eggs until the mixture has doubled in size, is pale, thick and creamy, and has reached 45°C (115°F) (a sugar thermometer is handy for this but otherwise use your finger and your best judgement – the mixture should feel like a very hot bath, and it takes roughly 2–3 minutes). Remove from the heat.

Gently fold in the flour bit by bit, until smooth. Line a baking tray with baking paper. Fill a piping bag with the batter (see note) and pipe fingers that are roughly 10 cm (4 in) long, 2.5 cm (1 in) wide and 1 cm (½ in) high. Leave 5–7 cm (2–2¾ in) between each finger (see note). If you like, dust with some icing sugar for a traditional look.

Bake for 6–8 minutes, or until the biscuits are puffed, golden and dry to the touch. Remove from the oven and let the biscuits cool completely on a wire rack, paper and all, before removing from the baking paper carefully.

>>

>> The biscuits are ready to be used immediately, but if you want to keep them for later I recommend letting them dry out on a wire rack overnight before packing into an airtight container. They will keep this way for 2 weeks.

Notes

A simple round 1 cm (½ in) nozzle will suit, but if you don't have a piping bag, something as simple as a zip-lock bag with the corner cut off will do the trick.

I find baking one tray of savoiardi at a time is best. To make twenty-four, fit about eight on each baking tray. They don't take long to bake, so while you have the first batch in the oven, you can pipe and prepare the next batch until you have three batches baked. Just remember to pipe the batter onto a cold baking tray. If you don't have three baking trays, you can quickly cool down the tray that has just come out of the oven by running cold water over it.

Torta *al* cioccolato

CHOCOLATE CAKE

I love looking through historic Italian cookbooks for interesting, even quirky, recipes, and I was lucky enough to make it the subject of a recipe column when I wrote for Italian newspaper *Corriere della Sera*. It was there where I first shared my love for this chocolate cake from Ada Boni's 1929 tome, *Il Talismano della Felicità*, also known simply as *The Talisman* in its highly abridged English versions.

When I first read the recipe it looked as though a mistake had been made – no eggs, no butter. It intrigued me immediately: a simple cake made with basic pantry staples, which would have been very convenient in Boni's time, between two world wars. It's an intensely deep, dark chocolate cake with a dense crumb, reminiscent of mud cake. Boni intends the cake to be served on its own, but I prefer it dressed up with a topping of Chocolate ganache (see page 119), some whipped cream and fresh berries for contrast, or with a dusting of icing (confectioners') sugar. It's also appealing because it is made with little fuss; you don't even need beaters – a spoon will do.

Boni's original recipe calls for more flour and less milk but I find it too stiff a batter. She also flavours it with cinnamon and orange zest; I prefer a pinch of salt and vanilla, or sometimes a freshly brewed shot of espresso. Being that it doesn't have egg and is easily made without dairy (see notes), this is a handy recipe to have up your sleeve if you're baking for anyone with a dietary restriction – or simply have a bare fridge and a craving for chocolate cake.

Preheat the oven to 180°C (350°F).

Grease a 20 cm (8 in) round cake tin and dust with sifted cocoa powder. Tap upside down to remove any excess.

Place the dry ingredients together in a bowl (do make sure the cocoa powder is sifted well to ensure you don't have problems with lumps later). Add the vanilla to the milk, then add this, bit by bit, to the dry ingredients, stirring with a wooden spoon until combined and smooth. If the batter is too stiff, you can add more milk (or even water).

Serves 6–8

100 g (3½ oz) Dutch (unsweetened) cocoa powder, sifted, plus extra for dusting

200 g (7 oz/1⅓ cups) plain (all-purpose) flour, sifted

200 g (7 oz) sugar

2 teaspoons baking powder

pinch of salt

1 teaspoon natural vanilla extract, or 1 vanilla bean, split lengthways and seeds scraped

350 ml (12 fl oz) full-cream (whole) milk (or alternative, see notes), or as needed

>> Pour into the tin and gently smooth the top. Bake for roughly 30 minutes, or until the centre of the cake feels springy to the touch and it smells cooked (see note) — it will be distinctly chocolatey.

When it has cooled enough to handle, remove from the tin and serve as desired — dusted with icing (confectioners') sugar or, when completely cooled, covered in ganache, perhaps with some berries on top or whipped cream on the side.

Notes

I've experimented with countless versions of this cake, especially making it dairy-free by replacing the milk with alternatives — I've tried it with almond milk and coconut milk (my personal favourite, as it makes a cake so buttery you would never guess it had none); coffee, which brings out the flavour of the chocolate beautifully (I go with a freshly made filtered coffee or an Italian-style moka coffee); and simply water (yes, it works!). I encourage you to experiment if you are interested in making this with other liquids; it is quite surprising how well it works. If you find the batter is slightly stiffer than you would expect you may need to add a little more liquid.

If you are using a larger cake tin, it will be slightly thinner and you may want to check the cake a little earlier to ensure you do not over-bake this cake.

A word on the cocoa powder. I use Dutch (unsweetened) cocoa powder, which is the most readily available type in Italy. In this process, the cocoa has been neutralised from its naturally acidic state, which makes it darker in colour, slightly more mellow in flavour, but also more soluble (for drinks such as hot chocolate). Importantly for baking, Dutch cocoa powder must be paired with baking powder rather than baking soda or bicarbonate of soda, which Ada Boni's original recipe calls for — as in many older recipes, she may have used natural cocoa powder, which is acidic and reacts with the baking soda to help the cake rise. You can also use natural cocoa powder here if it is all you have, but do not use baking soda in place of the baking powder if you are using Dutch cocoa powder. It's all about the chemistry.

Crostata *di* marmellata

APRICOT JAM TART

This is a classic recipe for the simplest jam tart pastry with an almost cake-like crumb. Both this jam recipe and pastry recipe are adapted from Pellegrino Artusi's 1891 cookbook, *Science in the Kitchen and the Art of Eating Well*.

    Crostata di marmellata is usually made with either blackberry or apricot jam. This silky smooth apricot jam is Artusi's own favourite out of all fruit jams and is also ideal for piping into home-made *Cornetti* (page 38) or *Bomboloncini* (page 48). You could substitute peaches for apricots, especially those blushing-rose peaches with yellow flesh. Otherwise, this tart can be made in a pinch with 250 g (9 oz) of your favourite ready-made jam and by simply following the recipe for the pastry crust.

Serves 8

JAM
500 g (1 lb 2 oz) ripe apricots
200 g (7 oz) sugar

SWEET SHORTCRUST PASTRY
125 g (4½ oz) cold unsalted butter
250 g (9 oz/1⅔ cups) plain
   (all-purpose) flour
80 g (2¾ oz) sugar
1 whole egg, plus 1 egg yolk, beaten
   (save the white to brush
   the pastry)
zest of 1 lemon

For the jam, halve the apricots and discard the pits. Put the apricot halves in a heavy-bottomed saucepan over a low heat, stirring occasionally so the fruit doesn't stick to the bottom of the pan. As the pan heats, the apricots will release their juices and the fruit will begin to simmer. Let the apricots simmer for approximately 30 minutes, stirring occasionally, or until the fruit is completely soft. Pass the mixture through a food mill or a fine-mesh sieve placed over a bowl to remove the skins for a smooth fruit purée.

Place the purée back in the saucepan over a low heat and add the sugar. Heat and stir until the sugar dissolves. Turn the heat up to medium and let it bubble until the jam reaches the consistency desired. If you let this go quite a while, you will get a harder-set jam, but even just a short 10 minutes will give you a nice soft-set jam, which is just right for this tart (see note).

For the pastry, chop the cold butter into small pieces. If using a food processor, pulse the butter, flour and sugar until you have a crumbly, sandy texture and there are no more visible pieces of butter. If mixing by hand, rub the butter into the flour and sugar until you achieve the desired result. Mix in the beaten egg and yolk along with the lemon zest until the pastry comes together into a smooth, elastic ball. Wrap tightly in plastic wrap and rest in the fridge for at least 30 minutes.

>>

>>   Preheat the oven to 180°C (350°F). Grease a 23 cm (9 in) pie dish.

Divide the dough into two pieces, one slightly larger than the other. Roll this larger piece out to about 3 mm (⅛ in) and press into the pie dish. Roll out the rest of the pastry and, with a pastry cutter or sharp knife, cut long strips about 2 cm (¾ in) wide. Fill the pie base with the jam and crisscross lattice strips over the top. If you like, use the leftover egg white to brush over the top of the pastry for some shine.

Bake in the oven for about 25 minutes, or until golden brown.

Note

The best test for the jam set is the frozen saucer test. Place a saucer in the freezer and when you want to test how set your jam is, place a teaspoon-sized blob of hot jam onto the cold saucer. Turn it sideways to see how it dribbles and wobbles. For me, this jam is ready when it slides slowly but decisively and wrinkles when poked.

Torta margherita

MARGHERITA SPONGE CAKE

Serves 6–8

4 eggs
120 g (4½ oz) caster
   (superfine) sugar
zest of 1 lemon or 1 vanilla bean
   (optional), split lengthways
   and seeds scraped
120 g (4½ oz) potato starch,
   sifted (see note)

Note
You can replace the potato starch
with cornflour (cornstarch), but do
not get potato starch confused with
potato flour. Potato starch is light,
powdery and 'squeaky' between
your fingers, exactly like cornflour,
whereas potato flour is simply
dehydrated, cooked potato ground
into flour – it is heavier and has
a texture similar to wheat flour.

Torta margherita is made light and fluffy with starch rather than
wheat flour, so it can take the place of *pan di spagna,* sponge cake
(for example, when making *Zuppa inglese*, page 146) and is handy
for those times when you need a gluten-free dessert. It can also be
enjoyed as is, simply paired with a dusting of icing (confectioners')
sugar and a good, strong coffee. The slices of pure-white coated cake
are said to resemble the white petals of a daisy, lending the cake its
name. Sometimes I add a bit of lemon or orange zest, or perhaps a
bit of vanilla, but I usually keep it very simple. Over the years, it has
been the cake I turn to for my daughters' birthdays – two of these
can be split into four layers to create an impressive, pillowy cake
that, when filled with an equally pillowy frosting of Italian meringue
(a soft meringue cooked over a bain-marie/double boiler), children
and parents alike love (and since we seem to often have guests who
can't eat dairy or wheat, this simple cake has always worked very
well for everyone to enjoy).

Preheat the oven to 180°C (350°F) and grease and line a 20 cm (8 in)
round cake tin.

Separate the eggs and beat the yolks together with the sugar until
very pale and creamy – like a sponge cake. The key here is to whip
for much longer than you think is probably necessary (Artusi tells his
nineteenth-century readers to whip for 30 minutes, though this would
have been by hand). If you want to add lemon zest or vanilla, add them
now. Sift in the potato starch and carefully fold through the batter
until smooth. The batter will become quite stiff.

In a separate, clean bowl, preferably glass or metal, whisk the egg
whites until stiff peaks form, then delicately fold the whites through
the batter, a little at a time at first, to loosen the batter. When just
combined, pour into the tin and bake until golden on top, and firm
and bouncy to the touch, about 30 minutes.

Torta di mele Apple cake/ *Torta di mele e marmellata* Apple and jam cake/ *Torta di limone e ricotta* Lemon and ricotta cake/ *Bocconotti* Little custard and quince jam pies/ *Budini di riso* Rice pudding pastries/ *Cornetti* Italian brioche croissants/ *Sfogliatine* Sweet puff pastries/ *Bomboloncini* Doughnut holes

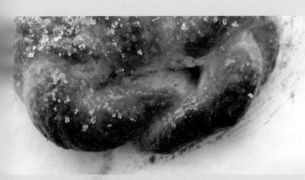

Colazione *all*'Italiana/

Italian breakfast

Start the day sweetly the Italian way, with flaky pastries just like the ones from the *pasticceria* and cakes made for dunking into oversized mugs of caffè latte.

Torta *di* mele

APPLE CAKE

This is one of those simple, homely cakes that you imagine everyone's nonna knows how to make and that you will always find, reassuringly, in bakeries, *bar* and pastry shops all over Tuscany. It's also commonly on *trattoria* menus for dessert, although many Tuscans eat this for breakfast or a mid-morning snack. It's not overly sweet, as Tuscans don't have much of a sweet tooth, but you could, if you like, brush a little warmed apricot jam (see page 23) over the top once you take it out of the oven for some shine and an extra touch of sweetness. Golden delicious apples are most commonly used in Tuscany for baking, but if you don't have them, use another good cooking apple, such as pink lady, granny smith or bramley (though the latter two are more tart, so the apricot jam or a dusting of icing (confectioners') sugar would be welcome).

Serves 8

2 large golden delicious apples (or other good cooking apple), peeled, cored and sliced 1 cm (½ in) thick
juice and zest of 1 lemon
180 g (6½ oz) sugar
125 g (4½ oz) unsalted butter, softened
3 eggs
150 ml (5 fl oz) milk
300 g (10½ oz/2 cups) plain (all-purpose) flour
1 teaspoon baking powder
pinch of salt

Preheat the oven to 180°C (350°F). Grease and line a 23 cm (9 in) round cake tin.

Place the apple in a bowl with the lemon juice and 2 tablespoons of the sugar.

Beat the remaining sugar with the butter until pale and creamy, add the eggs and beat very well until you have a thick, pale mixture. Add the milk and the zest, then fold in the flour, baking powder, salt and half of the apple slices, along with the lemon juice, to combine.

Pour into the tin and place the remaining apple slices all over the surface. Bake in the oven for 1 hour, or until the top is golden brown and springy to the touch.

Torta *di* mele *e* marmellata

APPLE AND JAM CAKE

This soft, buttery loaf cake, with chopped apple and apricot jam swirled through the top, is essentially a dressed-up pound cake (which Italians charmingly call a 'plum cake', using the English words but pronouncing the 'u' as 'oo'.)

Highly adaptable, this cake can be made in many different ways – just remember that the weight of the butter, sugar, eggs and flour should all be equal. I often combine polenta with the regular flour for a rustic cake with a good crumb, and sometimes I have made this with olive oil in place of the butter (use a little less, about 200 ml/ 7 fl oz). You can leave out the apple or exchange it for another fruit (pear, apricots, berries or plums would all be nice). Just don't skimp on whipping the eggs – it's what makes this cake so soft and fluffy without any other rising agents.

Serves 8

250 g (9 oz/1 cup) butter,
    at room temperature
250 g (9 oz) sugar
zest of 1 lemon
4 eggs, at room temperature
    (see page 8)
250 g (9 oz/1⅔ cups) plain
    (all-purpose) flour
1 apple, peeled, cored and diced
3 tablespoons apricot jam
    (see page 23)
icing (confectioners') sugar,
    for dusting (optional)

Preheat the oven to 170°C (340°F). Grease an 11 × 26 cm (4¼ × 10¼ in) loaf (bar) tin and line with baking paper.

Use an electric beater to cream the butter and sugar with the lemon zest until pale and creamy. Add the eggs one by one, beating well after each. Once all the eggs are in, beat continuously until very, very pale and fluffy. This takes about 7 minutes with electric beaters.

Fold in the flour carefully until it is just combined. Pour into the tin, drop in the diced apple and use a butter knife to gently swirl through the mixture to distribute. Smooth the top, then dollop the jam down the middle of the cake. Using a (clean!) knife pointing vertically down about 2–3 cm (¾–1¼ in) into the batter, swirl the jam in a zigzag pattern.

Bake for approximately 1 hour, or until it's golden on top and a wooden skewer inserted in the middle comes out clean. If the jam on top begins to look like it's darkening or cooking too quickly, you can cover the cake loosely with some aluminium foil. When cool, dust with icing sugar, if desired.

Serve in thick slices. When wrapped in plastic wrap and stored in the fridge, it will stay moist and fresh for 3–4 days.

Torta *di* limone *e* ricotta

LEMON AND RICOTTA CAKE

This classic *dolce casalingo* is the kind of home-made cake you would find sitting on a Tuscan kitchen counter. It's a sturdy cake with a good crumb, not too sweet or showy, with a subtle hint of lemon. The perfect vehicle for dunking, it's plain enough to make an ideal Italian breakfast, together with a deep, oversized mug of caffe latte.

Also known as the *torta del tre*, or the 'cake of three', it's a recipe I make a lot because it's quick and so very simple to remember (once you learn the main ingredients, you never really need to look at it again). It's also an extremely forgiving cake, so whether you make it round, rectangular or decide to add something new to it (a drizzle of lemon or rosemary icing, perhaps, see page 57), it's a nice one to have lying around at home, inviting children and adults alike to take thick slices of it with its simple, homely look.

Serves 8

3 eggs, separated
300 g (10½ oz) caster (superfine) sugar
300 g (10½ oz) ricotta (see note)
juice and zest of 1 lemon
300 g (10½ oz/2 cups) plain (all-purpose) flour
1½ teaspoons baking powder
3 tablespoons milk, or as needed

Preheat the oven to 180°C (350°F). Grease a 22 cm (8¾ in) round cake tin or an 11 × 26 cm (4¼ × 10¼ in) loaf (bar) tin and line it with baking paper.

In a clean, large bowl (preferably glass or ceramic), beat the egg whites with an electric beater until soft peaks form.

In a separate bowl, beat the egg yolks with the sugar and ricotta for 1–2 minutes, until creamy. Add the lemon juice and zest. Fold in the flour and baking powder and finally the egg whites.

Fold in the milk. Depending on the quality and firmness of your ricotta, you may find it is quite a dense batter – you may wish to add a splash more milk to loosen it.

Pour into the tin and bake for approximately 45–55 minutes, or until golden and springy on top. A skewer poked through the middle should come out clean.

Serve just as is with tea or coffee, for breakfast or as a snack. When wrapped in plastic wrap and stored in the fridge, it will keep for 3–4 days.

Note

Because this cake uses ricotta as the fat, rather than butter or oil, choose a full-fat ricotta for flavour and texture. Sheep's milk ricotta is preferable – it's a little richer, has more flavour and is more traditional than cow's milk ricotta in Tuscany. Try to buy ricotta that is very fresh, is made as traditionally as possible (in other words, from whey) and that can stand on its own.

Italian breakfast

Bocconotti

**LITTLE CUSTARD
AND QUINCE JAM PIES**

Makes about 8 pastries

1 egg, beaten (for the egg wash)
(optional)
icing (confectioners') sugar,
for dusting (optional)

JAM

500 g (1 lb 2 oz) quince, sliced
and cored but not peeled
juice of 1 lemon
½ vanilla bean, split lengthways
and seeds scraped
200 g (7 oz) sugar

CUSTARD

2 egg yolks
60 g (2 oz) sugar
20 g (¾ oz) plain (all-purpose) flour
250 ml (8½ fl oz/1 cup) milk, warmed

PASTRY

250 g (9 oz/1⅔ cups) plain
(all-purpose) flour, plus extra
for dusting
100 g (3½ oz) sugar
125 g (4½ oz/½ cup) cold butter,
diced
1 whole egg, plus 1 egg yolk, beaten
(save the white for the glaze)
finely grated zest of 1 lemon

In the pastry shops around Taranto in southern Italy and the province's white-washed towns, such as Martina Franca, you'll find such a dizzying array of *bocconotti* you won't even know where to start. Although they look simple enough from the outside, these little pies harbour fillings of custard, custard and sour cherries, sweet ricotta (on its own or studded with candied fruit, pieces of pear or chocolate), apple and cinnamon or jam. In Martina Franca, *bocconotti* – their name comes from the Italian word for 'mouthful', *boccone* – are often made with seasonal jams such as pear, quince or sour cherry, or are filled with custard or both custard and jam – my favourite. And if you're wondering how the *pasticcerie* can tell the difference between one filling and another, each pastry has a special code: some are glazed, some aren't but may have a dusting of icing (confectioners') sugar, others have a little hole or a 'button' of pastry on the top.

This is my favourite combination. Home-made quince jam makes a really special filling for its pretty pastel colour and unique perfume, but apple or pear are good substitutes (and they will only need about half the time to cook and to set). You can, of course, also use a store-bought jam of any flavour you like, but use the best quality one you can find.

For the jam, poach the quince in 750 ml (25½ fl oz/3 cups) simmering water until very soft, about 30 minutes. Drain and pass the fruit through a food mill or a fine-mesh sieve placed over a bowl. Place the purée back into the pot with the lemon juice and vanilla seeds and bring to a lively simmer. Add the sugar and cook until thick and set, about 30 minutes (see note on page 24).

To make the custard, whisk the yolks, sugar and flour until smooth in a small, heavy-based saucepan (see note). Add the warm milk, a little bit at a time, until smooth. Place the pan over a low heat and stir steadily with a whisk until thickened to a consistency like mayonnaise (it will thicken quite suddenly, so pay attention when it begins to change). Remove from the heat and pour the custard into a shallow bowl or dish. Cover with some plastic wrap, pressing down on the top of the custard (this is to prevent it from forming a skin), and set aside to cool.

34

>> For the pastry, combine the flour and sugar in a large bowl or in the bowl of a food processor. Add the cold butter pieces to the flour and sugar and, if using your hands, rub the butter into the flour until you get a crumbly mixture and there are no more visible butter pieces. If using a food processor, pulse until you have a crumbly texture. Add the whole beaten egg and the yolk to the flour mixture along with the lemon zest, then mix until the pastry comes together into a smooth elastic ball. Let it chill in the fridge, wrapped well in plastic wrap, for at least 30 minutes before using.

When you're ready to assemble the pastries, roll out the dough on a lightly floured surface until it is about 3 mm (⅛ in) thick. Cut out eight discs about 10 cm (4 in) in diameter (see note). Fill a muffin tin or ramekins with the pastry discs, pressing them down gently so they adhere to the bottom and sides perfectly. Prick the base several times with a fork.

Fill the pastries with about 2 heaped tablespoons of custard and 1 heaped tablespoon of jam, or until the pastry cases are almost full.

Gather together the leftover dough and roll it back out to a 3 mm (⅛ in) thickness. Cut out eight discs to cover the tops of the pastries, about 7–8 cm (2¾–3¼ in) in diameter.

Beat the leftover egg white and brush it over the edges of the pastries before putting the discs on top – this works like glue to seal the pastries nicely so the filling doesn't escape. Press down the edges very gently and, if desired, you can also mix up an egg wash with an egg plus 1 tablespoon of water to brush over the tops for a bit of shine. Otherwise, you can leave them plain and dust them with icing sugar once they've baked and cooled.

Bake at 180°C (350°F) for 20 minutes, or until the tops are golden brown and the pastry feels crisp. These keep well for a few days stored in an airtight container in the fridge, if not eaten immediately.

Italian breakfast

Notes

If you do not have a heavy-based saucepan or aren't confident about getting a very low heat out of your stovetop, you can use a bain-marie (double boiler; see page 10) instead. Mix the custard in a heatproof bowl set over a saucepan of simmering water and cook gently instead of directly on the heat.

For the measurements given in this recipe, I recommend using a standard muffin tin or individual ramekins with a 7–8 cm (2¾–3¼ in) diameter across the top, but if you already have something slightly different, adjust accordingly. For cutting the discs, you can use cookie cutters or a set of baking rings (which can also be known as cake, tart or mousse rings) in the appropriate sizes. Or you can do what a sensible nonna would: use whatever you have at home. You probably have a glass, mug or small bowl that is just the right diameter. Glasses can be pressed right into the dough like a cookie cutter, bowls and mugs with thicker rims can be flipped over and traced into the dough with a small, sharp knife.

You can make all parts of this recipe ahead of time; they all keep well for several days in the fridge and the pastry itself freezes very well.

Budini *di* riso

RICE PUDDING PASTRIES

Many say that the mark of a really good Florentine *pasticceria* is their *budini di riso*, a classic breakfast item among the line-up at any pastry shop. It's not that they are difficult to do. Actually, they are really quite easy. I believe it's more about the care put into them and the balance of sweetness, as it's so disappointing to get a sickly sweet *budino di riso*. The short pastry case should be thin, ever so slightly sweet and on the soft, blonde side. The rice pudding should be moist but firm, not hard and not too sweet, as the pretty, powdery icing sugar that coats the top supplies enough sweetness. To get the right shape, it's ideal to have a friand pan or deep, oval pastry cups. Failing that, you can simply use a regular muffin tin.

Makes about 8 budini

100 g (3½ oz) short-grain risotto
    rice, such as arborio or carnaroli
500 ml (17 fl oz/2 cups) milk
1 tablespoon unsalted butter
2 eggs, beaten
1 tablespoon sugar
pinch of salt
zest of 1 lemon
zest of 1 orange
1 teaspoon natural vanilla extract
1 quantity Sweet shortcrust pastry
    dough (see page 23)
icing (confectioners') sugar,
    for dusting

To make the rice filling, cook the rice and milk in a saucepan over a low–medium heat, stirring frequently until the rice is soft and the mixture is thick and creamy, about 20 minutes (keep a careful eye on it so that it doesn't overflow or burn). Take off the heat, add the butter and let it cool slightly before adding the eggs, sugar, salt, the lemon and orange zest and vanilla. Leave to cool completely.

Preheat the oven to 180°C (350°F).

After resting the pastry dough, place on a lightly floured work surface and roll out the pastry to a 2–3 mm (about ⅛ in) sheet. Cut out rounds and press into eight oval pastry cups or an eight-hole friand pan, leaving a few millimetres (about ⅛ in) of pastry overlapping the lip of the cup. Fill with the cooled rice filling.

Bake the budini for about 30 minutes, or until lightly golden and firm. Let them cool a little in the pan before cooling completely on a wire rack. Dust with icing sugar before serving. These are best eaten the day they are made (possibly warm) but you can store them in an airtight container in the fridge for a couple of days.

Cornetti

ITALIAN BRIOCHE CROISSANTS

Think of *cornetti* as Italian croissants but with a difference. They're less buttery (and therefore somewhat less flaky), more brioche-like (thanks to the addition of eggs) and, most importantly, they are always sweet, with a distinct citrus perfume. They're a staple of the Florentine *bar* counter or pastry shop and probably the most popular breakfast choice. You can find *cornetti* of all types: plain, wholewheat, dusted with icing sugar, shiny with sugar syrup, marbled with chocolate, or with a variety of fillings from jam to pastry cream to honey. Many *pasticcerie* will offer a selection of mignon pastries – that is, dainty half-sized ones, if you only want a small bite to eat.

This recipe, which is inspired partly by Paoletta Sersante's popular blog, Anice & Cannella, partly by Carol Field's method in *The Italian Baker* and partly by my own preferences, will give you small, *mignon cornetti vuoti* (or 'empty' cornetti) with a bit of shine from a lick of sugar syrup and some crunch from raw sugar. Once you've perfected these, you may like to try filling them by placing a teaspoon of your favourite jam (for example, see page 23) or other filling, such as Pastry cream (see page 16), on the widest part of the dough before rolling them.

While it looks like a lot of work, making *cornetti* is easier than it seems, mostly involving resting time to make this elastic dough easier to work with, and just a bit of rolling and folding in between. One piece of advice: it is best to work in a cool environment so that the butter doesn't get too soft, so resist the urge to make *cornetti* on a hot day. An ingenious tip I got from a pastry chef: if you have a warm kitchen, cover the work surface where you will be rolling your *cornetti* dough with a baking tray topped with ice or bags of frozen peas, and leave for a while to chill.

I like to make these over two or three days – it seems like a long time but it is very low maintenance this way and will easily fit around a work schedule. By the morning of the last day, which simply consists of shaping the *cornetti* and letting them rise before baking, you'll be rewarded with some of the best pastries you'll ever taste.

>>

>>

Makes about 20 small pastries

CORNETTI DOUGH
20 g (¾ oz) fresh yeast, or 7 g
   (¼ oz/2 teaspoons) active
   dry yeast
150 ml (5 fl oz) lukewarm water
75 g (2¾ oz) unsalted butter,
   softened at room temperature
50 g (1¾ oz) sugar
2 eggs
500 g (1 lb 2 oz/4 cups) strong
   (bread) flour (see note)
zest of 1 lemon
zest of 1 orange
1 teaspoon salt
250 g (9 oz) well-chilled unsalted
   butter (for the 'butter block';
   see note)
1 egg, beaten
raw (turbinado) sugar, for
   sprinkling (optional)

SUGAR SYRUP
45 g (1½ oz/3 tablespoons) sugar
3 tablespoons water

To prepare the dough, stir the yeast into the lukewarm water in a large bowl until dissolved. In a separate bowl, beat the soft butter into the sugar, add the eggs, then pour this into the yeast mixture and combine.

In a separate bowl, combine the flour, zest and salt. Stir the dry mixture bit by bit into the wet ingredients until the dough comes together (towards the end you may have to use your hands if not using a mixer).

Knead lightly on a floured work surface for 1 minute, or until the dough is smooth. Be careful not to over-knead or you will introduce too much elasticity. Put the dough into a bowl, cover with plastic wrap and let it rise for 1–1½ hours, or until doubled in size. Remove the dough from the bowl and knead a few times on a lightly floured surface to expel the air, then flatten into a disc. Double wrap the dough tightly in plastic wrap and refrigerate for 4–6 hours or overnight.

For the butter block, remove the well-chilled butter from the fridge 30 minutes before you need to use it. Place the butter between two sheets of baking paper and bash with a rolling pin until malleable but still cold, then shape it into a square roughly 12.5 cm (5 in) wide.

Roll out the dough to a rough square approximately 23 cm (9 in) wide and 1.5 cm (½ in) thick and place the butter in the centre of the dough at 45 degrees to its edges, so that the corners of the dough can fold perfectly over the edges of the butter block to enclose it like an envelope. Pinch and seal the dough well so that no butter escapes during rolling.

On a lightly floured work surface, roll this dough package forwards and backwards to create a long rectangle about 8 mm (¼ in) thick – the shortest side will be closest to you.

The next series of steps are known as 'turns' and consist of folding the rolled-out dough into thirds, turning the dough and rolling and folding again. If at any time it begins to get too difficult to roll the dough or the butter seems too soft, let the dough rest in the fridge for a short time, then try again.

For the first set of turns, fold the rectangle into thirds like a business letter: with the shortest side still closest to you, fold the top third down and the bottom third up. Turn the dough 90 degrees to the right (it should look like a book with the 'spine' to the left) and repeat: roll out the dough to a long rectangle 8 mm (¼ in) thick, then fold into thirds. Wrap the dough well in plastic wrap and chill for at least 30 minutes and up to 1 hour.

For the second and third pair of turns, repeat exactly as for the first set but after the third pair of turns, double-wrap the dough (so it does not explode out of the wrap as it gets the urge to rise!) and rest in the fridge for 4 hours or overnight, weighed down with a board or a plate and a few cans of beans or similar on top.

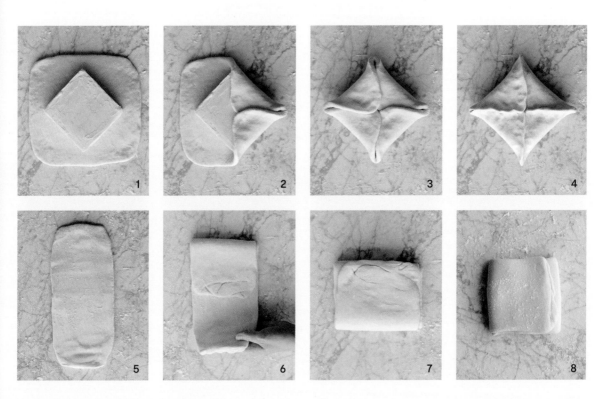

>>

To shape the cornetti, cut the dough into two even pieces. Keep one piece under a tea towel (dish towel), chilling in the fridge. On a floured work surface, roll out the other piece of dough into a rectangle about 20 cm (8 in) wide on one side and no more than 8 mm (¼ in) thick. With a very sharp knife or a pizza cutter, cut into two 10 cm (4 in) long strips, then cut each strip into even triangles with a base width of about 12 cm (4½ in). Trim any uneven edges with a knife. Dust lightly with flour if the dough begins to stick. Repeat with the rest of the dough and place unused pieces under a tea towel (dish towel) or loosely cover with plastic wrap to stop the dough from drying out while you shape the cornetti.

Position a triangle with the base towards you and very gently flatten and stretch the dough. To avoid ripping, pull from the centre outwards, not from the tips. Pull the top of the triangle up and stretch the base out wide towards the sides – you should be able to stretch the triangle to about double the height and to at least 17 cm (7 in) wide.

Once stretched, hold the tip of the triangle with one hand, and with the other roll up from the base to the top, keeping the tip stretched as you go. Tuck the tip underneath the cornetto, facing you. On a baking tray lined with baking paper, place the cornetti about 5 cm (2 in) apart to make room for rising (it is very difficult to move them after they have risen) and pull the ends into a crescent shape, bringing them together in front. Repeat with the rest of the dough.

Loosely cover the pastries with plastic wrap or a tea towel (dish towel) and let them rise in a warm place until doubled, about 2–3 hours.

Preheat the oven to 220°C (430°F).

When ready to bake, brush the cornetti delicately with the beaten egg.

Prepare the sugar syrup. Combine the sugar and water in a small saucepan and bring to the boil over a low–medium heat to dissolve the sugar. Set aside.

Put the pastries in the hot oven, then immediately reduce the heat to 200°C (400°F) and bake for 7–10 minutes, or until the cornetti are golden brown. Reduce further to 180°C (350°F) and continue baking until puffed and evenly browned, another 8 minutes or so. If the cornetti are darkening too quickly in the oven, remove them immediately and turn down heat or put them on a lower shelf. Once cooked, remove from the oven and place gently on a cooling rack.

Brush the cornetti with the sugar syrup while they are still warm. If desired, sprinkle some raw sugar over the top immediately after brushing with sugar syrup for a bit of crunch.

Notes

It's best to use a flour that will give the dough some strength (something with a protein content of about 12%) for successful stretching and shaping of the *cornetti*, so strong (bread) flour is ideal. In Italy it's common to use a combination of half Manitoba (strong) flour, which can have a protein content of 15–18%, and half '00' flour. If using only a weaker flour, such as plain (all-purpose) flour, you will risk the dough ripping when it comes to shaping or even rising. If you're not sure how strong your flour is, check on the nutrition label on the back of the packet and you should find the protein content.

In Italy, butter is unsalted and is very pale, sweet and creamy. If you can, try to use a cultured butter (also known as European-style butter). The difference is that it has a slightly higher fat content, which means it is more pliable (it won't crack when rolled, which can ruin all your hard work), and will create good flaky layers. Cultured butter also has a more complex flavour – all things that lead to better *cornetti*.

If you want to freeze any of the *cornetti*, do so directly after shaping. Freeze them on the baking tray covered in plastic wrap – when they're solid you can transfer them to freezer bags. To bake, place the frozen *cornetti* on a lined baking tray and thaw in the fridge overnight. The next day, let them rise in a warm place for 2 hours, or until doubled. Bake as described in the recipe.

Sfogliatine

SWEET PUFF PASTRIES

Also known as *borsettine* because they look like little coin purses, *sfogliatine* are available in many Florentine pastry shops. What really makes these special are the crunchy, slightly burnt-caramel bottoms made from rolling the dough over raw sugar as you prepare the pastries. Some are filled simply with pastry cream but others also feature sliced apple, rice pudding (such as in *Budini di riso*, page 37), jam or even chocolate. You can also keep them flat, somewhat oval shaped and open-faced. Top with pastry cream and cover with thin slices of apple – delicious!

Makes 18–20 small pastries

250 g (9 oz/1⅔ cups) plain (all-purpose) flour
1 teaspoon salt
250 g (9 oz) chilled unsalted butter (see note on page 43)
220 g (8 oz/1 cup) raw (turbinado) sugar
400 g (14 oz) Pastry cream (page 16)

The process for making this home-made puff pastry is similar to the one for Cornetti (page 38), but while cornetti dough is 'turned' three times, puff pastry is 'turned' six times.

Place the flour on a board and make a well in the centre of it. Add the salt and 150 ml (5 fl oz) water to the well and mix, slowly incorporating the flour around the water until you have a smooth dough. Let the dough rest in a bowl, covered, for 25 minutes.

Take the butter out of the fridge and let it soften slightly for 30 minutes while the dough is resting. To make the 'butter block', place the butter between two sheets of baking paper and bash it a little with a rolling pin to soften it and shape it into a square about 12 cm (4½ in) wide.

Roll the dough into a square about 20 cm (8 in) wide and about 1 cm (½ in) thick. For the following steps, see the photos on page 41. Place the square of butter in the centre of the square of dough at a 45 degree angle to the dough so that the corners of the dough can fold perfectly over the edges of the butter block, encasing it like an envelope. Pinch and seal the dough well. Let it rest for 10 minutes in the fridge, covered loosely with plastic wrap.

The next series of steps are known as 'turns' and consist of folding the rolled out dough into thirds, turning and rolling and folding again. If at any time it begins to get too difficult to roll the dough or the butter seems too soft, chill the dough in the fridge, then try again.

>>

>>   For the first pair of turns: roll the dough with a rolling pin on a lightly floured work surface to get a long rectangle (short side facing you), about 1.5 cm (½ in) thick. Fold like a business letter into three: fold the top third down and the bottom third up. Give the dough a quarter turn (90 degrees to the right; it should look like a book with the 'spine' to the left) and roll to a rectangle as before, i.e. 1.5 cm (½ in) thickness. You may find it harder to roll this time. Fold again the same way into thirds. Let it rest in the fridge, covered loosely, for 15 minutes.

Repeat another pair of turns and let the dough rest in the fridge for 15 minutes, loosely covered. Repeat three more pairs of turns, letting the dough rest in the fridge for 15 minutes, covered loosely, after each fold. Altogether you should perform six pairs of turns on the dough – this will ensure a flaky puff pastry.

To shape the sfogliatine, cut the dough into two pieces. Keep one portion covered in the fridge, and roll the other piece of dough out to a long rectangle of 2–3 mm (about ⅛ in) thickness. Roll the rectangle on the short side to create a long log. Cut the log into cylinders 4–5 cm (1½–2 in) long.

 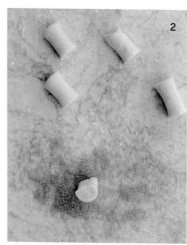 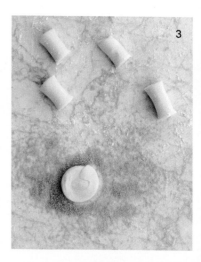

Notes

Use a setting that distributes heat equally from the top and bottom of the oven – or make sure you have an oven that cooks well from the bottom to begin with! You may need to put these on a low shelf to make sure that they cook well from underneath; otherwise, you risk undercooked pastry.

These pastries freeze very well. Prepare up until the point of baking and freeze on the baking tray, covered in plastic wrap. When frozen, you can remove the pastries from the tray and store in airtight plastic bags or containers, layered between greaseproof paper. When ready to bake, place the frozen pastries directly from the freezer onto a baking tray and immediately into a hot oven. Bake for an extra 15–20 minutes.

Dust the benchtop very lightly with flour and sprinkle over a generous amount of raw sugar. Stand each cylinder of dough upright and flatten the dough over the raw sugar with the palm of your hand to create a disc. Lightly dust with flour and roll the disc over the raw sugar from the centre upwards and downwards to obtain an oval shape approximately 1 mm (1/16 in) thick, 8–9 cm (3–3½ in) wide (in the centre) and 16–18 cm (6–7 in) long.

Place 1 level tablespoon of pastry cream on the bottom half of the oval, brush the edges lightly with water with the tip of your finger and fold the top half of the pastry over the filling. Place the pastry on a baking tray lined with baking paper. Loosely cover with plastic wrap, and continue working each piece of pastry in the same way until completed.

Preheat the oven to 200°C (400°F) (see note). Let the pastries rest in the fridge for 30 minutes, loosely covered. Bake for 10–15 minutes until the sfogliatine are golden and puffed, and the bottoms have caramelised.

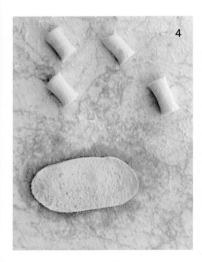

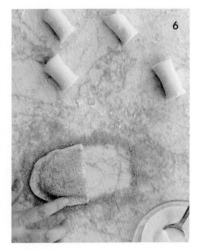

Bomboloncini

DOUGHNUT HOLES

The local *bar* near my mother-in-law's house is much like many in Italy. People gather there to chat, usually taking an espresso at the counter (standing, of course) or ordering trays of pastries to take home. The coffee's not great, but we don't really go there for the coffee. We go there for the *bomboloncini*. These innocently small round balls of light, sweet, fluffy dough – sometimes injected with pastry cream – are the perfect mouthful. We aren't the only ones who think so – by midday they're sold out. Somehow, even with an imperfect cup of coffee, that *bomboloncini* makes the morning.

A *bomboloncino* is a golf ball–sized version of the larger *bombolone*, the sort of pastry you'd find at every festival or market, freshly deep-fried from the back of a van. Many Tuscans have fond memories of eating *bomboloni* on the beach as a snack, or for breakfast on a Sunday morning, but you would never, ever eat these as a dessert after dinner.

Unlike many modern *bomboloni* recipes, which tend to be similar to *krapfen* (northern Italian–style doughnuts), this Tuscan version is its poorer cousin – more like a very soft bread dough deep-fried in vegetable oil. They are pillowy and somewhat lighter than the *krapfen*-style doughnuts, which contain eggs.

Dissolve the yeast in the water and let it sit for about 10 minutes. Combine the flour, 50 g (1¾ oz) of the sugar, the butter and salt in a bowl, and pour over most of the yeast and water mixture. Mix until it comes together. You may not need all the water, but you may need a dash more – this will depend on your flour and environment. Knead the dough on a floured work surface for about 8 minutes until it's no longer sticky and you have a soft and elastic ball. Put the dough in a bowl and cover with a tea towel (dish towel). Let it rise in a warm spot away from draughts for 2 hours.

Roll the dough onto a lightly floured work surface until it's about 1 cm (½ in) thick. Cut out circles with a little drinking glass or a small round cookie cutter – I use one about 5 cm (2 in) in diameter. Cut out rounds until you have used all the dough.

Makes about 16–18 small bomboloncini

15 g (½ oz) fresh yeast, or 7 g (¼ oz/2 teaspoons) active dry yeast
80 ml (2½ fl oz/⅓ cup) lukewarm water
200 g (7 oz/1⅓ cups) plain (all-purpose) flour
160 g (5½ oz) sugar
30 g (1 oz) melted unsalted butter
pinch of salt
vegetable oil, for frying
pastry cream (page 16) or jam of your choice (optional)

Italian breakfast

>>

>>

Heat the vegetable oil to 160°C (320°F) in a saucepan large enough for the bomboloncini to float (they shouldn't touch the bottom of the pan) (see note). Deep-fry in batches of three or four for 2 minutes on each side, or until deep golden and puffed. You can sacrifice your first one as a test to check that the inside is fully cooked. If not, you may need to turn down the heat ever so slightly and fry for a bit longer. Drain on paper towel for a moment, then immediately roll in the rest of the sugar and enjoy while still warm.

If you want to fill your bomboloncini with jam or pastry cream, use a metal- or plastic-tipped piping (icing) bag to squirt a small amount of filling inside each bomboloncino. If you don't have a piping bag, try doing this the way Pellegrino Artusi would have done in 1890 – simply place a teaspoon of jam on one disc of dough, moisten the edges with water, and sandwich another disc on top.

Note

Don't be put off by frying. Frying is easy. Just make sure to use a pot of oil deep enough that the dough floats while cooking, and be very careful with these *bomboloncini* as they fry at a relatively low temperature – about 160°C (320°F). To get that crisp, golden-brown exterior and fluffy interior, a sugar thermometer can be very helpful for monitoring the temperature, but if you're not sure of the temperature and don't have a thermometer, simply throw a cube of bread in the hot oil – it should turn golden in about 15 seconds.

Torta di nocciole Hazelnut cake/ *Ciambellone alle castagne* Chestnut flour bundt cake/ *Torta di mandorle di Nonna Vera* Nonna Vera's almond cake/ *Torta della nonna* Grandmother's tart/ *Crostata di ricotta e pere coscia* Ricotta and baby pear tart/ *Crostata di ricotta e cioccolato* Ricotta and chocolate tart/ *Mele al forno* Baked apples/ *Pesche ripiene* Stuffed peaches

Dal forno
di nonna/

From nonna's oven

The homeliest of desserts, including the
humble hazelnut cake, stuffed peaches
and ricotta crostata, are also some of
the most classic of all Italian sweets.

Torta *di* nocciole

HAZELNUT CAKE

Italians know that the best hazelnuts in the country come from Piedmont. Even more specifically, they come from the Langhe region, south of Turin, where this humble hazelnut cake was also born as an autumn and winter specialty – a way to use up excess nuts at the end of the season.

The classic *torta di nocciole* is dense with toasted hazelnuts, giving it a texture that is crumbly and even dry (a good excuse to pair some creamy *Zabaione* – page 152 – with it). Going slightly against tradition, I like to use raw hazelnuts that I pulverise in a food processor just before baking for a moister cake, rather than toasting the nuts or using store-bought hazelnut meal. Some like to include a spoonful or two of cocoa powder, but I prefer the nutty flavour of hazelnuts with just a splash of espresso added to the batter.

Serves 8

250 g (9 oz) raw, shelled hazelnuts
100 g (3½ oz/⅔ cup) plain (all-purpose) flour
1½ teaspoons baking powder
125 g (4½ oz/½ cup) butter, softened, plus extra for greasing
125 g (4½ oz) sugar
4 eggs, separated
60 ml (2 fl oz/¼ cup) freshly brewed espresso, cooled
125 ml (4 fl oz/½ cup) full-cream (whole) milk

Preheat the oven to 180°C (350°F) and grease and line a round springform cake tin approximately 23 cm (9 in) in diameter.

Pulverise the hazelnuts in a food processor until fine, like the texture of sand. Place in a large bowl with the flour and baking powder.

Beat the butter and sugar together in another mixing bowl until pale and creamy.

Whip the egg whites to stiff peaks. Add the yolks to the butter and sugar and mix. Next, add the dry ingredients, then the cooled espresso and milk, and stir with a spatula or wooden spoon until just combined. Finally, fold in the egg whites.

Gently pour the batter into the tin and bake for 30–35 minutes, or until the top is springy and deep golden brown – a skewer inserted into the middle of the cake should come out clean. Remove from the oven and leave to cool completely before removing from the tin. This cake keeps well for up to 3 days – store any leftovers in an airtight container or covered in plastic wrap in a cool place.

Ciambellone *alle* castagne

CHESTNUT FLOUR BUNDT CAKE

This ring-shaped cake is also known as *Ciambellone dell'Amiata*, referring to the use of chestnut flour from the volcanic Mount Amiata in southern Tuscany. It's an area well known for its chestnuts, which even have IGP (Indication of Geographic Protection) status, meaning they are recognised for their quality. The rosemary icing is my addition to this otherwise traditional cake. It gives the cake a pretty finish, and I love the flavour of rosemary in traditional Tuscan cakes and breads.

Serves 10

150 g (5½ oz) butter,
    at room temperature
200 g (7 oz) sugar
zest of 1 orange
4 eggs, at room temperature
150 g (5½ oz/1½ cups) chestnut
    flour, sifted
250 g (9 oz/1⅔ cups) plain
    (all-purpose) flour
1½ teaspoons baking powder
125 ml (4 fl oz/½ cup) milk
2 tablespoons rum (optional)

ICING
1 tablespoon rosemary,
    leaves picked
50 g (1¾ oz) icing (confectioners')
    sugar, sifted
2 teaspoons warm water

Preheat the oven to 170°C (340°F). Grease a 25 cm (10 in) ring (bundt) tin with melted butter or olive oil. Tip in some flour and tap the tin to distribute a very fine, even layer all over the inside of the tin. Set aside.

Use an electric mixer to cream the butter and sugar with the orange zest until pale and creamy. Add the eggs one by one, beating well after the addition of each.

Combine the flours and baking powder in a bowl and fold these dry ingredients into the batter carefully, alternating with the milk, until just combined. Add the rum (if using) and fold through carefully. Pour the batter into the tin.

Bake in the oven for about 30 minutes, or until golden on top and a wooden skewer inserted in the middle comes out clean. Remove and let the cake cool in the tin before turning out onto a plate. You can eat it simply like this or, for a non-traditional addition, you can try adding my light, runny rosemary-scented glaze. Simply rub the rosemary into the icing sugar, then stir through just enough warm water to make it quite runny, about 2 teaspoons. Drizzle over the cake.

Variations

You can use 125 ml (4 fl oz/½ cup) of olive oil in place of the butter, or lemon zest instead of the orange zest. The milk can be replaced with water to make this recipe dairy-free. Instead of the rum, you can use brandy or any aniseed-scented liqueur, or leave it out altogether.

Torta *di* mandorle *di* Nonna Vera

NONNA VERA'S ALMOND CAKE

This is a solid, foolproof recipe, easy to remember and so easy to whip up (all you need is a bowl and a fork) – practical, just like Nonna Vera, my husband's paternal grandmother, who is in her mid nineties. It's a cake that my mother-in-law, Angela, has made countless times, bringing it to every meeting or gathering she was ever invited to, even inventing a summer version where she leaves off the almonds and instead tops the cooked cake with fresh strawberries macerated in sugar and whipped cream – she thinks of this almond cake as decidedly wintry, but I like it at any moment, especially with an espresso.

Serves 6–8

150 g (5½ oz/1 cup) plain
    (all-purpose) flour
150 g (5½ oz) sugar
150 g (5½ oz) butter, melted
1 whole egg, plus 3 egg yolks
finely grated zest of 1 lemon
100 g (3½ oz) blanched whole
    almonds
icing (confectioners') sugar,
    for dusting

Combine the flour and sugar in a bowl. Pour over the melted butter and mix. Add the egg and yolks one at a time, and then the lemon zest, stirring with a fork.

Preheat the oven to 180°C (350°F) and grease and line a 20 cm (8 in) round cake tin. Pour the cake batter into the tin and top with the whole almonds, pushing them in slightly.

Bake for 30 minutes, or until golden brown on top. Dust with icing sugar to serve.

Torta *della* nonna

GRANDMOTHER'S TART

This is a classic custard tart that is said to have been invented by Florentine chef Guido Samorini after his customers complained they were tired of the usual trattoria dessert offerings. Today it's a much-loved dessert that all Florentine pastry shops make and many *trattorie* still offer. It requires a few different steps, such as preparing the shortcrust pastry and pastry cream, but it is actually a very simple and lovely dessert made out of relatively little. There is even a 'grandfather's' version of this tart, *torta de nonno*, which is made with a Chocolate pastry base (just add 50 g/1¾ oz cocoa powder to the dough) and Chocolate pastry cream (see page 117), and is basically, in Carol Field's words, 'Chocolate pudding tucked in a soft, buttery crust.' You can substitute slivers of blanched almonds for the pine nuts if you wish.

Serves 8

50 g (1¾ oz/⅓ cup) pine nuts
1½ quantities Sweet shortcrust
   pastry dough (see page 23
   and note)
1 quantity Pastry cream (page 16)
   with the zest of 1 lemon added
milk or water, for brushing
icing (confectioners') sugar,
   for dusting (optional)

Preheat the oven to 180°C (350°F).

Soak the pine nuts in cold water for 10 minutes, then drain. This will stop them from burning in the oven.

After resting the pastry dough, roll out two-thirds of the dough and line a 23 cm (9 in) pie dish. Place a sheet of baking paper over the top of the pastry and place weights such as baking beads (or uncooked rice or dried beans) on top. Blind bake for 10 minutes, then remove the beads and let the pastry cool.

Fill the cooled pie crust with the pastry cream.

Roll out the rest of the dough to about 2 mm (1/16 in) thick and place over the top of the tart, trimming the edges. This will shrink a little so leave about 5 mm (¼ in) extra overhang and seal. Brush the top with milk or water and scatter with the drained pine nuts.

Bake for 40 minutes, or until the top is golden brown.

When cool, dust with icing sugar (if desired) and serve at room temperature.

Note

This recipe requires one and a half quantities of the shortcrust pastry. I find it easiest to just double the pastry recipe and save the leftovers for making mini tarts or even simple cut-out cookies. It also freezes well so you can save it for later.

Crostata *di* ricotta *e* pere coscia

RICOTTA AND BABY PEAR TART

Ricotta crostata is a favourite dessert in Southern Tuscany, which borders the region of Lazio. Popular versions are the ones dotted with chocolate chips (see page 65) or layered with lip-smacking sour cherry jam or compote made from *visciole*, sour cherries, a well-known dessert of Rome's old Jewish ghetto.

I have always loved the combination of ricotta and pear, and came up with this version that uses poached baby pears (known as *pere coscia* in Italian) – yellow skinned, a little firmer and crunchier than regular pears – which can be found all over the local farmers' markets around Tuscany in the summer. This very simple dessert is not overly sweet and is pretty enough to present to guests. Once baked, the tart is best when left to settle overnight in the fridge and eaten the next day – chilled if it's summer, and room temperature otherwise.

Peel the baby pears. Leave the stems on (I don't core them, as they are so small and tender they don't need it). Slice about 5 mm (¼ in) off the bottom of the pear, so that they have flat bottoms to sit on. Roughly chop the pear offcuts and leave aside to add to the ricotta mixture. If you're making this dish with regular-sized pears, peel and slice them into quarters and remove the core (if they are particularly large pears, you can slice into eighths).

Slide the pears into a saucepan of simmering water (just enough to cover the pears) with the sugar to add a touch of sweetness to them. Cook for 15 minutes, or until they are just tender. Remove the pears, drain and let them cool.

To make the pastry, combine the flour, sugar and butter in a bowl. Using your fingers, rub together until there are no more visible pieces of butter (or you can pulse in a food processor). Add the salt and egg plus yolk and combine until it comes together into a smooth ball. Wrap in plastic wrap and put in the fridge to rest for 30 minutes, then roll out on a lightly floured surface to about 3 mm (⅛ in) thick. Lay over a 22–25 cm (8¾–10 in) round pie dish and trim the edges. Prick the surface gently all over with the tines of a fork (see note).

Preheat the oven to 180°C (350°F).

Serves 8

icing (confectioners') sugar, for dusting (optional)

POACHED PEARS
7–9 baby pears (see note)
55 g (2 oz/¼ cup) sugar

PASTRY
250 g (9 oz/1⅔ cups) plain (all-purpose) flour
100 g (3½ oz) caster (superfine) sugar
125 g (4½ oz/½ cup) cold butter, chopped
pinch of salt
1 whole egg, plus 1 egg yolk

FILLING
500 g (1 lb 2 oz/2 cups) ricotta
100 g (3½ oz) caster (superfine) sugar
zest of 1 lemon
1 teaspoon natural vanilla extract, or ½ vanilla bean, split lengthways and seeds scraped
2 eggs

From nonna's oven

>> To make the filling, combine the ricotta, sugar, lemon zest, vanilla and eggs, and mix until smooth. Pour the filling over the pastry-lined pie dish and smooth over. Carefully push the pears into the ricotta filling, then bake in the oven for 45 minutes, or until the top is firm, slightly golden brown and the pastry crust is golden.

Let it cool completely before serving and, if you like, just at the last moment sprinkle over some icing sugar – this will mostly sink into the surface of the ricotta and the pears, so you won't see much of it, but it will add a hint of sticky sweetness.

Store this tart in the fridge and eat within 2–3 days.

Notes

If you can't find baby pears, you can make this with regular pears. Choose firm rather than ripe pears, which hold their shape better. This tart would work nicely with halved and pitted apricots or plums (though these would not need to be poached).

If you have some leftover pastry, roll out to make mini tart bases that you can blind bake in a muffin tin or cut out cookies that you can decorate with icing or layer with jam. It's a versatile dough that also freezes very well – nice to have for a rainy-day baking project.

Crostata *di* ricotta *e* cioccolato

RICOTTA AND CHOCOLATE TART

Serves 8

icing (confectioners') sugar,
  for dusting (optional)

PASTRY
250 g (9 oz/1⅔ cups) plain
  (all-purpose) flour
100 g (3½ oz) caster (superfine)
  sugar
125 g (4½ oz/½ cup) cold butter,
  chopped
pinch of salt
1 whole egg, plus 1 egg yolk

FILLING
500 g (1 lb 2 oz/2 cups) ricotta
170 g (6 oz) caster (superfine) sugar
2 eggs
2 tablespoons rum
finely grated zest of 1 lemon
  or orange
80 g (2¾ oz) dark chocolate, finely
  chopped (or chocolate chips)

Variations
Substitute the chocolate with rum-soaked raisins, and add a thick layer of sour cherry jam beneath the ricotta. You could also add 50 g (1¾ oz) unsweetened cocoa powder to the pastry.

Dotted with chocolate pieces, this classic ricotta tart is almost like stracciatella gelato, and scented with a hint of rum. It's a simple tart, but you could easily make little adjustments to tailor it to your taste.

To make the pastry, combine the flour, sugar and butter together in a bowl. Using your fingers, rub together until there are no more visible pieces of butter (or you can pulse in a food processor). Add the salt and egg plus yolk and combine until it comes together into a smooth ball. Wrap the pastry in plastic wrap and put it in the fridge to rest for 30 minutes, then roll out on a lightly floured surface to about 3 mm (⅛ in) thick.

Press the dough into a 22 cm (8¾ in) round springform cake tin and trim the sides to about 4 cm (1½ in) high, reserving the excess pastry. Prick the surface gently all over with the tines of a fork. Roll out the rest of the dough into a rectangular shape, 3 mm (⅛ in) thick, and cut long strips with a fluted pastry roller or sharp knife. Set aside.

Preheat the oven to 180°C (350°F).

To make the filling, combine the ricotta, sugar, eggs, rum and citrus zest, and mix until smooth. Add the chopped chocolate, then fill the dough-lined cake tin with the mixture and smooth over. Use the long strips of dough to make a crisscross lattice top. Trim the edges with a sharp knife so that you have an even border and where the lattice meets the sides of the tart, press the edges down well to seal.

Bake in the oven for about 45 minutes, or until the top is firm and well-browned and the pastry crust is golden. Let it cool completely before serving. In fact, I like this best when it has even had a bit of time to be chilled. If you like, just before serving, dust the top of the tart with icing sugar.

Store this tart in the fridge and eat within 2–3 days.

Mele *al* forno

BAKED APPLES

You'll find these baked apples in the homeliest of Tuscan trattorie during autumn and winter, served warm, just as they are with their sugar-crusted tops and sticky bottoms. I am partial to cream or Zabaione (page 152) on a warm, freshly baked apple, and they're even great cold the next day with a blob of thick natural yoghurt.

Use a good cooking apple for this, and preferably something slightly tart (otherwise halve the sugar if using a sweet variety). Pine nuts or crumbled walnuts are also a very good addition to the filling.

Serves 4

60 g (2 oz/½ cup) sultanas or raisins
4 medium organic, unwaxed cooking
  apples
50 g (1¾ oz) butter
60 g (2 oz) sugar
splash of white wine, vin santo
  or rum (optional)

Preheat the oven to 180°C (350°F).

Soak the sultanas in hot water until plump, about 15 minutes. Rinse and core the apples but leave the skins on.

Lightly butter a small baking dish with half of the butter. Place the cored apples in the dish, fill the holes with the sultanas and sprinkle the sugar over evenly. Pour about 1 cm (½ in) water into the bottom of the pan and add a splash of wine, vin santo or rum, if desired. Bake for 30–40 minutes, or until soft and cooked through (test with a skewer), basting the apples from time to time with the liquid in the bottom of the baking dish, which will eventually turn into a delicious syrup. Let them cool slightly, then serve warm with some syrup dribbled over.

Pesche ripiene

STUFFED PEACHES

This is simply one of the most wonderful summer desserts of all time: nothing more than baked halved peaches stuffed with crushed amaretti biscuits, eggs and sugar. You can find this Piedmont classic in all of Italy's most important historic cookbooks, from Pellegrino Artusi's *Science in the Kitchen and the Art of Eating Well* to Ada Boni's *Il Talismano della Felicità*.

Artusi calls for a filling of Savoiardi (page 17) with freshly pounded almond meal (useful to try if you don't have amaretti biscuits). Boni mentions they can be served warm or cold, while De Giacomi and Lodi's Langhe cookbook, *Nonna Genia*, includes cocoa powder and insists they must be served warm or tepid, never cold. I personally love the addition of chocolate to the almond and peach combination, but rather than put it in the filling I like a little dark chocolate shaved on top. They are quite delicious with some Zabaione (page 152).

Serves 6

7 medium yellow peaches
   (see note)
1 tablespoon sugar (optional;
   see note)
5 amaretti biscuits, crushed
   (see note)
1 egg yolk
1–2 tablespoons butter,
   plus extra for greasing
dark chocolate, shaved,
   to serve (optional)

Preheat the oven to 180°C (350°F).

Rinse the peaches and pat dry. Cut six of the peaches in half, removing the pits and scooping out some extra pulp from each half to make room for the filling. Finely chop this extra pulp and place in a small mixing bowl.

Peel the last peach, then mash or finely chop (depending on how tender the flesh is) the fruit and add it to the bowl, along with the sugar (if using), the amaretti biscuit crumbs and the egg yolk, and combine well.

Place the peach halves, face up, in a well-buttered baking dish large enough to fit the twelve halves in a single layer. Fill the peaches with the amaretti mixture and top each with a dot of butter. Bake until the peaches are cooked through, oozing a pretty coloured juice and nicely browned on top, about 40 minutes.

Serve warm or tepid, with some shaved chocolate over the top if you like.

From nonna's oven

Notes

Use ripe but not overly mature peaches here; the latter can lose their shape while cooking and become too soft. If using particularly sweet peaches and quality amaretti, you may find you can get away with not using sugar in this recipe.

There are two types of amaretti made with essentially the same ingredients of sweet almonds, bitter almonds (which give these little biscuits their name: amaro means 'bitter' in Italian), egg whites and sugar. *Amaretti di Saronno,* which come from Lombardy, are smaller, hard and crunchy, while *amaretti di Sassello* from Liguria are softer, blonder, almost cake-like biscuits that often come individually wrapped. Both are only just over the Piedmont border, but it's more common to use *Amaretti di Saronno* for this recipe.

Pandiramerino Rosemary and sultana buns/ *Schiacciata all'uva* Grape focaccia/ *Torcetti* Sweet breadsticks/ *Cioccolato e pane* Grilled chocolate sandwich/ *Fiori di acacia fritti* Fried acacia (black locust) blossoms/ *Frittelle di ciliegie* Cherry fritters/ *Fichi canditi* Caramelised figs/ *Ricotta con miele di fichi* Ricotta with fig honey

Merende dolci/

Sweet snacks

These treats, from fried acacia blossoms
to Florentine raisin and rosemary buns,
are perfect for a little pick-me-up in
those in-between times.

Pandiramerino

ROSEMARY AND SULTANA BUNS

Shiny and delightfully sticky with decorative split, crisscrossed tops, *pandiramerino* – which means 'rosemary bread' (*ramerino* is the charming Tuscan word for *rosmarino* or rosemary) – are fragrant with fresh rosemary and studded with sweet sultanas (golden raisins). Traditionally these rustic buns were made for *giovedì santo*, the Thursday before Easter, and were without sultanas, hence their name. Now you find them year round in bakeries all over Florence.

Makes 8 buns

20 g (¾ oz) fresh yeast,
  or 7 g (¼ oz/2 teaspoons)
  active dry yeast
1 tablespoon sugar
180 ml (6¼ fl oz/¾ cup) lukewarm
  water
300 g (10½ oz/2 cups) plain
  (all-purpose) flour, sifted
70 g (2½ oz) sultanas (golden raisins)
2 rosemary sprigs, chopped
  (about 1 tablespoon)
60 ml (2 fl oz/¼ cup) extra-virgin
  olive oil, plus extra for brushing
pinch of salt
55 g (2 oz/¼ cup) sugar

Combine the yeast, sugar and water in a mixing bowl and let it sit for 10 minutes until dissolved. Pour over the sifted flour and combine to make a firm ball of dough. Place the dough in a lightly greased bowl, cover with plastic wrap or a tea towel (dish towel) and let it rise in a warm place away from draughts for 1 hour.

Meanwhile, put the sultanas, rosemary and oil together in a bowl and set aside to infuse until the dough has risen.

Combine the dough with the sultanas, rosemary, oil and salt. Work the ingredients together by kneading, and divide into eight small balls weighing approximately 70–80 g (2½–2¾ oz) each. Place the buns on a baking tray lined with baking paper and cover loosely with a tea towel (dish towel). Allow the buns to rise for a further 30 minutes.

Preheat the oven to 200°C (400°F).

Brush the tops with olive oil and slash a tick-tack-toe grid (similar to a hash symbol) over each one with a very sharp knife or razor. Let them rest another 10–15 minutes, then bake in the oven for 20 minutes.

Meanwhile, prepare a sugar syrup by dissolving the sugar in 2 tablespoons of water in a small saucepan and bringing to the boil. Take off the heat and brush the hot buns with the hot syrup.

The buns are best eaten the day they are made, but they will keep well for 1–2 days in an airtight container.

Schiacciata *all'*uva

GRAPE FOCACCIA

Born in and around the wine-growing areas of Florence and the Chianti, this delicious bread is a tradition governed by the very seasonal nature of grapes in Italy, and one that also has an extremely close tie with the wine harvest in autumn.

For one or two fleeting months of the year from September to October, the appearance of *schiacciata all'uva* in Florence's bakery shop windows is a sign that summer is over and the days will begin to get noticeably shorter. This sticky, sweet focaccia-like bread, full of bright, bursting grapes, is a hint that winemakers are working hard at that moment harvesting their grapes and pressing them. And then, as suddenly as it appeared, the grape focaccia is gone, not to be seen again until the following September.

These days, it is usually made with fragrant, berry-like concord grapes (*uva fragola*) but sometimes you'll still find it made with native Tuscan wine grapes known as *canaiolo* – the small, dark grapes make up part of the blend of Chianti wine, playing a supporting role to sangiovese. These grapes stain the bread purple and lend it its juicy texture and sweet but slightly tart flavour. They are also what give the bread a bit of crunch, as traditionally the seeds are left in and eaten along with the bread.

Serves 6–8

500 g (1 lb 2 oz/3⅓ cups) plain (all-purpose) flour, plus extra for dusting
20 g (¾ oz) fresh yeast, or 7 g (¼ oz/2 teaspoons) active dry yeast
400 ml (13½ fl oz) lukewarm water
75 ml (2½ fl oz) extra-virgin olive oil, plus extra for greasing
600 g (1 lb 5 oz) concord grapes (or other black grape; see note)
80 g (2¾ oz) caster (superfine) sugar
1 teaspoon aniseed (optional; see note)
icing (confectioners') sugar (optional)

You can prepare the dough the night before you need to bake it, or a couple of hours ahead of time.

Sift the flour into a large bowl and create a well in the centre.

Dissolve the yeast in about 125 ml (4½ fl oz/½ cup) of the lukewarm water.

Add the yeast mixture to the centre of the flour and mix with your hand or a wooden spoon. Add the rest of the water little by little, working the dough well after each addition to allow the flour to absorb all the water.

Add 1 tablespoon of the oil to the dough and combine.

>>

This is quite a wet, sticky dough. Rather than knead, you may need to work it with a wooden spoon or with well-oiled hands for a few minutes until it is smooth. Cover the bowl of dough well with some plastic wrap and set it in a warm place away from draughts until it doubles in size, about 1 hour. If doing this the night before, leave the dough in the bowl to rise in the fridge overnight.

To assemble the schiacciata, separate the grapes from the stem, then rinse and pat dry. There's no need to deseed them if making this the traditional way (see note).

Preheat the oven to 190°C (375°).

Grease a 20 × 30 cm (8 × 12 in) baking tin or a round pizza tray with olive oil. With well-oiled hands, divide the dough into two halves, one slightly larger than the other. Place the larger half onto the greased pan and, with your fingers, spread the dough out evenly to cover the pan or so that it is no more than 1.5 cm (½ in) thick.

Place about two-thirds of the grapes onto the first dough layer and sprinkle over half of the sugar, followed by about 30 ml (1 fl oz) of olive oil and ½ teaspoon of the aniseed, if using.

Stretch out the rest of the dough to roughly the size of the pan and cover the grapes with this second layer of dough, stretching to cover the bottom surface. Roll up the edges of the bottom layer of dough from underneath to the top, to seal the edges of the schiacciata. Gently push down on the surface of the dough to create little dimples all over. Cover the top with the rest of the grapes and evenly sprinkle over the remaining aniseed, sugar and olive oil.

Bake for about 30 minutes, or until the dough becomes golden and crunchy on top and the grapes are oozing and cooked.

Allow to cool completely. Cut into squares and enjoy eaten with your hands. If you like, dust with icing sugar just before serving – although this isn't exactly traditional, it is rather nice.

This is best served and eaten the day of baking, or at most the next day.

Notes

Avoid using seedless table grapes or white grapes for this – they just don't do it justice in terms of flavour or appearance. If you can't get concord grapes or wine grapes, or it's the wrong season, try replacing them with blueberries. It's completely unorthodox, of course, but it's a very good substitute, giving you a much closer result than using regular table grapes.

There are rarely adaptations made to this traditional recipe, but often you can find the addition of aniseed – a typical Tuscan flavouring for sweets – as I've suggested here. It's a good addition, one that brings extra perfume to this bread.

Torcetti

SWEET BREADSTICKS

First recorded in dessert cookbooks from the late 1700s, it's said *torcetti* were born in the old communal wood-fired ovens of the countryside north of Turin, the capital of Piedmont, where they were once made as a special treat to keep children occupied while the adults busied themselves with the bread baking.

These flaky, crumbly breadsticks are rolled in sugar, twisted into a drop shape and baked until they get sticky, caramelised bottoms. After the first time I tasted them in Turin, I couldn't walk past a bakery without stopping to get a bag of *torcèt*, as they're known in dialect.

I suggest doing the second rise overnight – pop the dough in the fridge and let the second rise work while you're sleeping. The next morning, the buttery dough – thanks to the chill of the fridge – is also easier to handle. But the best reason for doing this is so that you have warm torcetti to dip into your morning coffee without having to wake up too early.

Makes about 50 torcetti

18 g (½ oz) fresh yeast or 7 g (¼ oz/ 2 teaspoons) active dry yeast
250 ml (8½ fl oz/1 cup) lukewarm water, or as needed
500 g (1 lb 2 oz/3⅓ cups) plain (all-purpose) flour, plus extra for dusting
100 g (3½ oz) sugar
pinch of salt
170 g (6 oz) unsalted butter, softened (see note on page 43)

Place the yeast in a small bowl with about 60 ml (2 fl oz/¼ cup) of the lukewarm water to soften.

Put the flour in a large bowl with 2 tablespoons of the sugar and the salt. Add the yeast mixture and as much of the remaining water as you need to bring the flour together to a soft, but not sticky, dough. Knead lightly for a few minutes, then put the dough back in the bowl, cover the top of the bowl loosely with plastic wrap or a tea towel (dish towel) and leave to rise in a warm place in the kitchen for 1 hour.

In the meantime, dice the butter and beat with an electric mixer for a few minutes until creamy.

Add the butter to the risen dough and knead or mix until well incorporated. It may be sticky at this point and, if excessively sticky, you can add some extra flour until you have a soft and manageable dough. Place the dough back in the bowl, cover as before and leave to rise for an hour or so in a warm spot, or until doubled in size. You can also leave the bowl of dough in the fridge overnight and finish the shaping in the morning (I highly recommended doing this).

>>

If you have done the second rising in a warm spot, give the dough a feel. If it is very soft and sticky, chill the dough in the fridge for 30 minutes – this will help harden the butter to make handling easier. If it is still too sticky to work with, add a little more flour.

Place the rest of the sugar on a surface where you can roll pieces of dough, such as a large, flat plate or directly on a clean chopping board, pastry board or kitchen surface.

Preheat the oven to 200°C (400°F).

To begin with, on a very lightly floured surface roll out about half of the dough into a rectangular shape, ideally about 10 cm (4 in) long and 1 cm (½ in) thick. With a large, sharp knife, cut the dough into 1 cm (½ in) strips and roll each in the sugar to lightly but evenly coat. Try to stretch the dough out to double the length so you have long 'snakes'. Bring the ends together and pinch into a drop shape. Place on baking trays lined with baking paper. Continue with the rest of the dough.

Bake in batches, for 12–15 minutes, or until light golden brown. Enjoy warm while you can, but leave to cool completely before storing torcetti in a biscuit tin or airtight container.

Notes

Torcetti are at their best the day they're baked, but if making this amount seems like too much to get through, you can halve the dough, double wrap it in plastic wrap and freeze it (for up to 6 months) while the rest has its second rise. When ready to use, let the dough come back to room temperature and continue the recipe from the second rise.

You can keep torcetti for a few days and reheat in a low oven to bring back their crunch.

Cioccolato
e pane

**GRILLED CHOCOLATE
SANDWICH**

This is basically a sweet version of the favourite Italian snack known simply as 'toast', which is actually a toasted white bread ham and cheese sandwich. I first had it at Turin's beautiful Caffè Il Bicerin where, sitting on a red velvet bench with Billie Holiday playing in the background, a single flickering candle on the table, and with a glass of their eponymous *bicerin* (a decadent drink of hot chocolate and coffee smothered in whipped cream), I have enjoyed the sweetest treats I have ever had. Although it's not quite the same eating this at home, it is, even in its simplicity, so wonderfully decadent. The key is to use Turin's famous *gianduiotto* chocolate, which is a velvety, creamier-than-usual hazelnut chocolate that comes wrapped up like miniature gold bars. Failing that, use the best-quality chocolate you want to treat yourself to.

This is normally made with square sandwich bread, which children would probably be overjoyed with. But, if you're making this as a treat with very nice chocolate, I have to say, it's even more delicious with your favourite proper bread. Crusts on or off, it's up to you.

Serves 1

knob of butter, softened
2 slices bread
50 g (1¾ oz) gianduiotti or other
   favourite, quality chocolates
   (about 5), chopped

Butter one side of each slice of bread. Sandwich the chocolate between the unbuttered sides, then toast or grill (broil) on an electric sandwich press or simply in a hot pan with a weight on the sandwich. Toast until the bread is golden and crisp outside, and inside the chocolate is melted — you will need a few minutes on each side.

Fiori *di* acacia fritti

**FRIED ACACIA (BLACK
LOCUST) BLOSSOMS**

For a short couple of weeks in late spring, maybe even less, the country roads of Tuscany are lined with thin trees bearing bunches of pretty white flowers. Hanging down like miniature chandeliers, they have a heavy intoxicating perfume, quite like jasmine or orange blossom. You can't miss them. Known as black locust trees (or false acacia, *Robinia pseudoacacia*) in English, they are native to North America and were brought to Europe in the early 1600s. In Italy they go by the name acacia.

This recipe is similar to fried zucchini flowers (courgette or squash blossoms), which are really just a vehicle for eating deliciously crisp, fried batter – but with black locust blossoms, you have a delicate flavour of nectar and spice mingling with that perfume reminiscent of orange blossom. They can be dusted in icing (confectioners') sugar or – my favourite – drizzled with locust honey (also known as acacia honey), a pale, delicate and fragrant honey.

You can use this same batter for frying other edible blossoms, such as wisteria and heads of blooming, fragrant elderflower (*Sambucus nigra*), which overlap the black locust season in Tuscany.

Serves 4

150 g (5½ oz/1 cup) plain
    (all-purpose) flour
12 large bunches of acacia
    (black locust) blossoms
vegetable oil, for frying
icing (confectioners') sugar,
    for dusting, or 1 tablespoon
    honey

Whisk the flour and 250 ml (8½ fl oz/1 cup) water together in a large bowl until smooth. Let it rest and chill in the fridge for at least 30 minutes. The batter should be smooth and fairly runny – it should run off a spoon quickly. You may find after the resting time that you need to add a little more water.

In the meantime, prepare the flower bunches by trimming off any leaves and cutting into separate bunches. Leave the stem a good 4–5 cm (1½–2 in) long – it's handy for dipping and pulling the bunch out of the oil. Do not wash them (see tips).

Pour the oil into a medium saucepan until it's about 4–5 cm (1½–2 in) deep – enough oil for the flowers to float in. Place the pan over a medium–high heat and bring the oil to a temperature of about 160°C (320°F). You can use a sugar thermometer or test with the end of a wooden spoon – the spoon should be surrounded immediately by

lots of tiny bubbles as soon as it hits the oil. If the oil starts smoking, it's too hot – turn down the heat or remove from the heat to cool it down for a moment.

Fry in batches of three or four so that you don't overcrowd the pan. Dip a bunch of flowers into the batter and turn to coat evenly. Holding the bunch by the stem, let the excess batter run off the flowers for a moment. Still holding the stem (tongs can do this if you're not game with fingers), place in the hot oil, shaking a little for the first few seconds so that the flowers separate from each other. Cook, turning as needed, for about 30–60 seconds, or until the batter is crisp and evenly pale golden.

Drain on paper towel and continue dipping and frying with the rest of the bunches. Serve the warm fried flowers with a dusting of icing sugar or a drizzle of honey.

Tips for foraging and preparing flowers

- Take a pair of secateurs and a basket for the flowers. Avoid polluted areas, such as roadsides.
- Go in the morning when flowers are freshest.
- Smell before you pick. Keep only the best smelling flowers, as these will also be the best tasting ones. Avoid wilted or old flowers and don't pick flowers right after the rain.
- Eat only the flowers and not the stems or leaves, which in some cases are toxic, but for ease of preparing, cut the flowers with stems intact.
- Don't wash the flowers, as they can lose their fragrant pollen. However, do check for insects.

Frittelle *di* ciliegie

CHERRY FRITTERS

Makes about 24 fritters

200 g (7 oz/1⅔ cups) plain
    (all-purpose) flour
3 teaspoons baking powder
120 g (4½ oz) sugar
zest of 1 lemon
pinch of salt
1 egg
180 ml (6 fl oz) full-cream
    (whole) milk
splash of Alchermes (see page 8)
    or rum (optional)
200 g (7 oz) fresh cherries,
    pitted and roughly chopped
vegetable oil, for frying

Note

These fritters should be fried rather
slowly so that they cook all the way
through – if the temperature is too
high, they will brown too quickly and
remain raw inside. I suggest sacrificing
the first one or two fritters by looking
inside to ensure they are cooked
through to the centre. Once you
have the temperature stabilised and
the timing right, frying these fritters
is a cinch. It is a good idea to scoop
out any little drops of batter that
have fallen into the oil before they
burn, and to replenish the oil about
halfway through.

In the Tuscan hilltop town of Lari, in the Pisan countryside, cherries
have been cultivated for centuries. Once a year, on the verge of
summer, nearly twenty native varieties of cherry can be sampled at
the town's cherry festival. At the festival's market you can find not
only fresh cherries, piled high in baskets, but also cherry delicacies,
from pies to liqueurs to jams – there's even cherry-scented beer.
But, by far, most popular is the stall where a team of nonne diligently
whip up a paddling pool–sized bowl of batter and deep-fry fresh
cherry fritters in an equally giant pot of bubbling oil. This is how
I recreate them at home.

Place the flour, baking powder, 2 tablespoons of the sugar, the lemon
zest and salt in a mixing bowl. Stir together briefly, then add the egg
and milk, whisking until you have a smooth batter, rather like pancake
batter. Add a splash of Alchermes, if using, and stir through the cherries.

Place the rest of the sugar in a small bowl (I prefer something shallow).

Pour enough oil into a small–medium saucepan so that the fritters
can float. Heat over a medium heat to 160°C (320°F), or until a cube
of white bread dropped into the oil turns golden brown in about
15 seconds.

Give the batter a stir in case the cherry pieces have fallen to the
bottom, then drop a tablespoon of batter into the hot oil and fry
evenly, turning to cover all sides, until deep golden brown, about
2½–3 minutes (see note). They will puff-up into walnut-sized fritters.
Aim to cook several at a time, in batches. Transfer the cooked fritters
to a wire rack lined with paper towel to drain the excess oil for
a moment before rolling the fritters, still hot, in the sugar. These
are best eaten warm, right away.

Fichi canditi

CARAMELISED FIGS

This is a delicious and elegant way to preserve fresh figs whole, in syrup. It's a little like fig jam, only with less sugar and rather than a mush of figs, here they are barely touched, so they are beautifully and perfectly whole.

Caramelised figs are rather special with soft cheeses as part of a cheese platter, or with good fresh ricotta, natural yoghurt or just stolen right out of the jar, as is. You can also make them a tiny bit boozy by adding a splash of Cognac or other brandy to the syrup once taken off the heat.

In southern Tuscany, green figs (which seem to grow everywhere and anywhere, rising out of stone walls or cracks in the concrete) are most common, but you could use any fig for this. Just make sure they aren't bruised, split or overly ripe. In fact, this is a good recipe for slightly under-ripe figs — they hold their shape very well when cooked this way.

**Makes 2 × 250 ml
(8½ fl oz/1 cup) jars**

1 kg (2 lb 3 oz) figs
peel of 1 lemon (organic or
    unwaxed), in long strips (you
    can use a vegetable peeler)
200 g (7 oz) sugar
splash of Cognac or other
    brandy (optional)

The night before, rinse the figs carefully and place them tightly together, bottoms down, in an even layer in a heavy-bottomed pot (one that you would use for jamming). If you need to make two layers, just make sure the figs are still carefully sitting upright. Add the strips of lemon peel, pour over the sugar and leave it overnight in a cool place.

The next day, place the pot over a gentle heat and let them cook slowly, uncovered, and without stirring. After about 20 minutes of simmering, the figs will begin to soften. At this stage, try to carefully nudge them into one layer, still upright. I use a large spoon for this; be careful so as not to accidentally pierce them.

Continue simmering until the figs are covered in syrup. When cooked, they should be entirely soft (including their stems) and evenly caramel coloured, and the syrup should be producing big bubbles as it boils. The timing depends entirely on the figs themselves — what kind they are, the thickness of their skins, their level of maturity. It can take about 1 hour, but keep an eye on them.

>>

Carefully lift out each boiling hot fig and place in clean, sterilised jars (see note). If you want to make them boozy, add a splash of Cognac or other brandy to the syrup now. Then pour the syrup over to cover the fruit completely, until 5 mm (¼ in) from the top. Seal the lids tightly – but don't turn them over or re-boil them to seal. Just let them sit on the counter until thoroughly cooled. Store in the fridge.

When sealed properly, the unopened jars of figs last for several months. Once opened, store in the fridge and consume within a week. (They never last that long though!)

Note

There are two ways to sterilise jars. In Italy, they like to put the jars, mouths up, along with their lids (not screwed on, but left off) in a large pot covered with water, then boil them for 10 minutes. Remove jars and lids (I do this with tongs) to air-dry on a clean tea towel (dish towel), jar mouths up. You can also sterilise jars in the oven. Wash the jars with warm, soapy water. Place them, mouths up, on a baking tray in a low oven until dry. The lids should be boiled for 10 minutes and left to air-dry on a tea towel (dish towel).

Ricotta *con* miele *di* fichi

RICOTTA WITH FIG HONEY

Fig honey isn't actually honey but a heady syrup made from boiling dried figs. It has the same consistency and golden caramel colour of wild honey. It also has similarities to *vincotto*, or cooked grape must, which has been used in the south of Italy as a honey and sugar substitute for centuries — both feature in traditional baked goods or are drizzled over fried pastries such as *cartellate* or *pettule*.

Fig honey is easy to make and can be conserved for a long time — even years. You can put it on anything you like, from toast to roasted pork (it makes a great glaze), but the way I like to enjoy it is on good ricotta — the kind that was made fresh that morning and can stand on its own. Keep it as an indulgent treat for yourself, or top it with chopped walnuts or almonds and you have a simple dessert for friends and family.

This makes about 180 ml (6 fl oz) of fig honey, which is more than enough for this recipe, but it's not a bad idea to have extra on hand for drizzling over everything. Save any leftovers in a jar and store in the fridge or somewhere cool.

Serves 4

400 g (14 oz/1½ cups) dried figs
400 g (14 oz) fresh farmer's ricotta, to serve

Note

You won't need the fig pulp anymore but don't discard it — it's lovely stirred through thick yoghurt, used in cakes, or as a filling for pastries such as *Bocconotti* (page 33) in place of jam.

Slice the figs in half and put them in a saucepan with 1 litre (34 fl oz/ 4 cups) water. Let them soak until completely soft and plump. If using dried figs that are particularly dry, you can leave them to soak overnight in the fridge.

Place the saucepan over a low heat and gently simmer for about 1 hour, or until the liquid is reduced by about half. Strain the figs and their liquid in a muslin (cheesecloth)-lined sieve set over a bowl.

When the figs are cool enough to handle, bring the edges of the muslin together and give it a good squeeze and a twist to extract as much liquid as you can. Place the strained liquid back into the pan and bring to the boil (see note). Reduce the heat and simmer gently for a further 30–40 minutes, or until reduced by another half. It should look like a thick syrup or honey and smell caramelised. Set aside to cool.

To serve, divide the ricotta between four bowls and drizzle a few spoonfuls of fig honey over the top.

Cantuccini Almond biscotti/
Ciambelline al vino Red wine biscuits/
Tozzetti Ebraici Jewish cinnamon
biscotti/ *Corolli rossi* Red crown
biscuits/ *Zuccherini* Aniseed biscuits/
Paste di meliga Polenta biscuits

Biscotti/

Biscuits

These classic Italian biscuits are made to last and are best when dunked in coffee, tea, or even wine.

Cantuccini

ALMOND BISCOTTI

Tuscan dinners most often end with a plate of almond-studded *cantuccini* accompanied by the local dessert wine, vin santo (perhaps home-made), poured into small tumblers, with much dunking, drinking, eating and lingering. It's the quintessential element that rounds off any meal, whether it is shared among new or old friends at home or offered by friendly and generous trattoria hosts.

In Tuscany they are known as *cantuccini* – often named after Florence's neighbour and the city of their invention, Prato – but they are better known as biscotti (the general Italian word for 'biscuits') in the English-speaking world. The word *biscotti* comes from the fact that these biscuits are twice ('*bis*') cooked ('*cotto*'), a technique that Pliny the Elder once said would make baked goods keep for centuries. They are first shaped into a sort of flat log, baked, then cut into slices and baked again. The double baking makes them durable, crunchy and perfect for dipping into vin santo or coffee.

Makes about 36 biscotti

125 g (4½ oz) whole almonds, chopped roughly in half
350 g (12½ oz/2⅓ cups) plain (all-purpose) flour
200 g (7 oz) sugar
1 teaspoon baking powder
pinch of salt
2 whole eggs, plus 1 egg yolk for glazing
30 ml (1 fl oz) vin santo
1 tablespoon honey

Preheat the oven to 180°C (350°F).

Place the almonds on a baking tray and toast for 10 minutes in the oven, then let them cool.

Combine the dry ingredients in a large bowl. Make a well in the centre and crack the eggs in (reserve the extra yolk for glazing later). Add the vin santo and honey (warmed, if not runny enough) and beat the wet ingredients with a fork, slowly incorporating the dry ingredients around them until it becomes a dough. Add the almonds and continue mixing with your hands until the dough is well combined.

Shape the dough into thin logs, about 2 cm (¾ in) high, 4 cm (1½ in) wide, and slightly flattened. Place on baking trays lined with baking paper, at least 5–8 cm (2–3 in) apart.

Beat the extra egg yolk and brush the tops and sides of the logs with the beaten egg. Bake in the oven at 180°C (350°F) until golden, about 20–25 minutes. Turn the oven down to 130°C (270°F).

>> When just cool enough to handle, slice the logs at a 45 degree angle into 1.5 cm (½ in) slices (use a sharp, heavy kitchen knife that can easily chop through nuts).

Place the cantuccini on their sides back onto the baking tray, and bake for a further 20 minutes, or until crisp and dry to the touch (but not coloured).

These biscuits keep well when stored in an airtight container – if they are not eaten all at once.

Variations

The recipe for *cantuccini* has thousands of variations. While the one I use is adapted from my mother-in-law's recipe, it is quite different from the very first nineteenth-century recipe for *biscotti di Prato*, which included pine nuts and did not have any raising agents.

If you do not have vin santo on hand, you could substitute another dessert wine or even rum. Otherwise, simply leave it out.

You can replace the almonds with an equal amount of large chunks of dark chocolate (as pictured on page 94). Leave the logs to cool completely before slicing and only do the second baking just before serving so you can serve the biscotti warm, with the chocolate just melting.

Ciambelline *al* vino

RED WINE BISCUITS

Delicate and simple, these lovely biscuits are made for dunking into wine, but go just as well dunked into coffee or tea. They're really perfect anytime and seeing as they're made with just a few pantry staples – flour, sugar, olive oil and wine – they can be whipped up at any moment.

They can be made with red or white wine or, if you don't like wine, you can replace it with milk. If you have it, a splash of aniseed-scented liqueur is commonly used, too.

Makes about 40 biscuits

500 g (1 lb 2 oz/3⅓ cups) plain (all-purpose) flour
150 g (5½ oz) sugar, plus extra for topping
½ teaspoon baking soda
125 ml (4 fl oz/½ cup) extra-virgin olive oil
125 ml (4 fl oz/½ cup) red wine

Use your hands to make a soft dough by combining the flour, sugar, baking soda, olive oil and wine together until smooth.

Preheat the oven to 180°C (350°F) and line one or two baking trays with baking paper, depending on size.

Roll 1 tablespoon of dough into a log a little wider than your palm – about 12 cm (4¾ in) long and 1 cm (½ in) thick. Bring the ends to meet and, overlapping slightly, press gently together to seal the rings.

Put a few tablespoons of sugar in a small shallow bowl or plate and press each ring face down into the sugar. Place on the baking tray about 2 cm (¾ in) apart from each other.

Bake for 20 minutes, or until pale golden and dry to the touch. Remove from the oven and let them cool on a wire rack.

These will keep for several weeks when stored in an airtight container in a cool, dark place.

Tozzetti Ebraici

JEWISH CINNAMON BISCOTTI

I first tasted these delicious, cinnamon-scented *tozzetti Ebraici* or 'Jewish *tozzetti*' at the Forno del Ghetto, a bakery at the mouth of the old ghetto in Pitigliano, a stunning town in Tuscany's deep south, historically one of the most important in the region for its Jewish community. Although there is no longer a Jewish community in Pitigliano, a handful of Jewish traditions have survived here, namely *Sfratti* (page 128), Pitigliano's best-known baked good; *pane azzimo* (unleavened matzo or matzah bread); and these *tozzetti*.

In the biscotti world, almond-studded *Cantuccini* (page 9) are the best known, especially in northern Tuscany, around Florence and in Prato, the town where they were born. In southern Maremma, they are called *tozzetti*, no doubt a tradition that has seeped over the nearby borders of Lazio and Umbria, where *tozzetti* are also common. They're all similar, of course, but tozzetti are usually made with hazelnuts instead of almonds because they are more commonly available. And then there are *mandelbrot* (meaning 'almond bread'), – Jewish cookies that look remarkably similar to classic Tuscan *cantuccini*, so much so they could be cousins. I can't help but imagine that *tozzetti Ebraici* are the result of mandelbrot and rustic Maremman *tozzetti* coming together within the ancient stone walls of Pitigliano. The main feature of *tozzetti Ebraici* is the cinnamon – there's enough to give these biscotti that hint of coppery brown colour and to perfume the whole house when you pull them out of the oven.

Beat together the eggs and sugar. Add the oil and blend until creamy. Add the flour, baking powder, cocoa powder and cinnamon, and combine to form a dough. If it's too sticky to handle, carefully add a little more flour. You should have a soft dough. Add the lemon zest and nuts towards the end.

Preheat the oven to 180°C (350°F) and line two baking trays with baking paper.

Makes about 50 biscuits

3 eggs
250 g (9 oz) sugar
125 ml (4 fl oz/½ cup) extra-virgin olive oil
470 g (1 lb 1 oz) plain (all-purpose) flour, plus extra for dusting
1 teaspoon baking powder
2 teaspoons unsweetened cocoa powder
2 tablespoons ground cinnamon
zest of 1 lemon
200 g (7 oz) whole, peeled hazelnuts

With floured hands, divide the dough into six portions and roll these into thin logs, about 2.5 cm (1 in) wide. Place them on the baking trays with plenty of space between them.

Bake in the oven for 20 minutes. They should appear dry and firm, usually cracked along the top but not browned. Remove from the oven, let them cool for several minutes until you can handle them, and slice with a heavy, sharp knife (not a serrated knife) into biscotti about 1.5–2 cm (½–¾ in) thick. Return the sliced biscotti to the oven to dry out ever so slightly, about 5 minutes.

Thick and chunky, these are just the thing for dunking into a cup of tea, coffee or dessert wine.

Corolli rossi

RED CROWN BISCUITS

I often bought these pretty pink cookies from the local bakery when I lived in Porto Ercole in southern Tuscany so I always had something to serve with coffee to visiting friends. Soft and crumbly and smelling of spices, they're traditionally made with lard and lots of eggs, and perfumed with citrus zest. The bright pink pop of colour comes from Alchermes, a Florentine liqueur (see page 8).

The name *corollo* comes from the Latin *coronula*, which refers to a crown of flowers. These little crowns are also the name of a similar, ancient Sienese pastry, which had the distinct fragrance of aniseed. It was common for *corolli* or other similar, ring-shaped biscuits, to be strung up with a piece of string and hung like an edible garland across the counter, tempting customers to pluck them off to have with their coffee.

Makes about 36 biscuits

400 g (14 oz/2⅔ cups) plain
    (all-purpose) flour
200 g (7 oz) sugar
zest of 1 lemon
1 teaspoon baking powder
3 eggs, beaten
60 g (2 oz/¼ cup) melted butter,
    cooled

TOPPING
125 ml (4 fl oz/½ cup) Alchermes
    (see page 8)
200 g (7 oz) sugar

Combine the flour, sugar, lemon zest and baking powder in a large bowl. Add the eggs and butter and mix to make a firm dough. If you find it's a little crumbly, add a splash of the Alchermes (or some water).

Preheat the oven to 180°C (350°F) and line one or two baking trays with baking paper, depending on size.

Roll 1 tablespoon of dough into a log about 14 cm (5½ in) long. Bring the ends together and, overlapping slightly, press gently together to seal the ring. Continue making rings until you have used all the dough.

Place them on the baking tray (or trays) about 4–5 cm (1½–2 in) apart from each other and bake for 20 minutes, or until they are puffed and pale golden. Remove from the oven and cool on a wire rack.

Pour the Alchermes into a small, shallow bowl. Put about a quarter of the sugar in another small, shallow bowl. Dip each cooled corollo face down first in the Alchermes (just halfway), then into the sugar. (The drips of liqueur will create an even finish on the cookies.) Place them on a tray to dry. As the sugar gets used up, top with fresh sugar.

These will keep for several weeks when stored in an airtight container in a cool, dark place.

Zuccherini

ANISEED BISCUITS

Nonna Maria, my husband's great-grandmother, was responsible for the baked goods at the alimentari and *bar* that she and her husband, Angiolino, ran in the middle of Fucecchio (a Tuscan town halfway between Florence and Pisa). She was a sturdy countrywoman with the arms of someone who doesn't complain one bit about stirring a giant pot of polenta for an hour, breaking chicken necks, or plucking little black birds while everyone else looks away.

Her *zuccherini* were well known, so much so that not only did they become the only true specialty of Fucecchio, but the only bakery that still produces them today, each *Carnevale* (Carnival) season in February, uses her recipe. The large, sweet, blonde rings of aniseed-flavoured biscuit were traditionally strung on a pole to hang in the pantry and were meant to last until Lent. As they are baked for a short time, they retain quite a soft, crumbly interior. They're perfect broken into small pieces to dip into coffee.

Makes 8 large zuccherini

350 g (12½ oz/2⅓ cups) plain (all-purpose) flour, plus extra for dusting
1½ teaspoons baking powder
200 g (7 oz) sugar
2 teaspoons aniseed, whole
2 eggs
1 tablespoon honey
zest of 1 lemon
1½ tablespoons sassolino, sambuca or other aniseed-flavoured liqueur (or milk)

Preheat the oven to 180°C (350°F).

Combine the dry ingredients in a bowl, make a little well in the middle and crack in the eggs, adding the honey, lemon zest and alcohol. Begin mixing the eggs into the dry ingredients with a fork at first, then you will have to use your hands to bring it together to a soft dough. Wrap in plastic wrap and chill the dough in the fridge for about 30 minutes.

On a lightly floured surface, divide the dough into two pieces and, working one piece at a time, roll the dough into a long log, about 2.5 cm (1 in) thick. Cut into lengths about 22 cm (8¾ in) long and join the ends together to produce large rings. Transfer them to one or two baking trays lined with baking paper (leave plenty of room between the biscuits) and, with a sharp knife, make fairly deep, decorative indentations across the surface of the biscuits. Continue with the rest of the dough.

Place the baking tray(s) in the middle rack of the oven and bake for 12–15 minutes, or until the biscuits are only very lightly browned on the top and bottom. They will still feel slightly soft when you take them out of the oven, but will harden a little as they cool. They will last a long time stored in a cool, dry place in an airtight container.

Paste *di* meliga

POLENTA BISCUITS

In the homely trattorie of the city of Turin, Piedmont's capital, these ancient and deliciously crumbly polenta biscuits (*meliga* means *mais*, or corn, in local dialect) are offered with a glass of moscato or dolcetto at their simplest, or with a bowl of creamy, freshly whipped *Zabaione* (page 152, and pictured opposite) at the end of the meal. The Count of Cavour, a native Piedmontese, is said to have requested at the end of every meal two *paste di meliga* with a glass of Barolo Chinato, a herby, digestive dessert wine. A real treat.

Preheat the oven to 180°C (350°F).

Combine the polenta, flour and sugar in a mixing bowl. Add the chopped butter and process in an electric mixer or, using your hands, rub the butter into the dry ingredients until the mixture resembles breadcrumbs.

Add the lemon zest, egg and yolk and mix until smooth and creamy. The consistency should be thick, but quite wet – enough to put into a piping (icing) bag (even a makeshift one, such as a zip-lock bag). Cut a hole to allow piping the batter in a width of 1 cm (½ in), or use a large enough piping nozzle (this is done with a star-shaped nozzle in Turin's bakeries). Pipe rings about 5–6 cm (2–2½ in) in diameter directly onto one or two baking trays lined with baking paper. Bake for 15 minutes, or until the biscuits appear dry on the top and very lightly golden.

If you are not eating them right away, they will store well in a sealed biscuit tin for up to 2 weeks.

Note
Look for the finest ground polenta you can get – in Italy you would use a type of polenta called *fioretto*, which is most often used for baking (it is pale yellow and as fine as flour), rather than the coarser type used for making cooked, soft polenta.

Makes about 22 biscuits

100 g (3½ oz/⅔ cup) fine polenta (see note)
100 g (3½ oz/⅔ cup) plain (all-purpose) flour
75 g (2¾ oz) sugar
125 g (4½ oz/½ cup) butter, chopped
finely grated zest of 1 lemon
1 whole egg, plus 1 egg yolk

Schiacciata alla Fiorentina Florentine cake/ *Torta di Nonno Mario* Nonno Mario's cake/ *Torta di pera e cioccolato* Pear and chocolate cake/ *Tronco al cioccolato* Chocolate-filled sponge roll/ *Torta di semolino e cioccolato* Semolina and chocolate tart/ *Cavallucci* Spiced walnut biscuits/ *Cenci* Sweet deep-fried pastry/ *Sfratti* Honey and nut pastries/ *Frittelle di riso* Rice fritters/ *Pagnottella* Fig and chocolate bread

Per festeggiare/

For celebrations

Desserts for special occasions, whether it's just to impress, or to carry on the age-old regional traditions of Christmas and *Carnevale* (Carnival) time.

Schiacciata *alla* Fiorentina

FLORENTINE CAKE

In February each year, around *Carnevale* (Carnival), there's no avoiding it – the scent of orange peel and vanilla wafts through the cold late winter air and you can't go past a pastry shop in Florence without noticing that the windows are filled with large, flat, sugar-dusted yeasted cakes known as *schiacciata alla Fiorentina*. Traditionally served plain, but often filled with sweet, freshly whipped cream or pastry cream, they're instantly recognisable for the *giglio* (the Florentine fleur-de-lis and symbol of the city of Florence) masked and dusted over the top in contrasting powdered cocoa. The characteristic flavour (marked by orange zest) and incredibly soft, spongy texture make it a favourite for a mid-morning or afternoon snack or even breakfast with coffee. It also goes down quite nicely with a glass of vin santo or dessert wine.

Although it requires a long rising time, this cake is easy to make. You could leave it simple with just a dusting of icing (confectioners') sugar. But the hint of bittersweet cocoa goes so well with the subtle orange scent of this cake, you'll want to offer the slice that has the *giglio* on it to your favourite person.

Serves 6

20 g (¾ oz) fresh yeast, or 7 g (¼ oz/2 teaspoons) active dry yeast
150 ml (5 fl oz) lukewarm water
300 g (10½ oz/2 cups) plain (all-purpose) flour, plus extra for dusting
100 g (3½ oz) lard (or, less traditional, butter), softened
100 g (3½ oz) sugar
1 whole egg, plus 2 egg yolks
zest of 1 orange
1 teaspoon natural vanilla extract
pinch of salt
icing (confectioners') sugar, for dusting
unsweetened cocoa powder, for dusting (optional; see note)

Prepare a 20 × 30 cm (8 × 12 in) baking tin by greasing and dusting with flour.

Dissolve the yeast in the water in a mixing bowl and let it sit for about 10 minutes.

In a large bowl, mix the flour with the yeast mixture until just combined. Cover with a tea towel (dish towel) and place in a warm, dry spot to rise for about 1 hour, or until the dough has doubled in size.

In a separate bowl, beat the lard, sugar, egg and yolks, orange zest, vanilla and salt very well until the mixture is pale and creamy. Add this to the dough, combining thoroughly until you have a smooth and creamy mixture. Place the dough in the baking tin. The dough should be about 2 cm (¾ in) high. Cover with some plastic wrap and let it rise for 2 hours.

Preheat the oven to 180°C (350°F).

>>

For celebrations

>>   Bake for 25–30 minutes, or until the surface is firm and golden brown
        and a skewer inserted in the middle comes out clean. Turn onto a wire
        rack to cool. When cooled completely, dust liberally with icing sugar.

Notes

If you want an authentic look, cut out a paper mask of the Florentine lily and
carefully dust over the top of the icing sugar with contrasting cocoa powder.

If you want to make this simple cake a little more substantial, slice through the
middle of the cake and fill with some slightly sweetened, freshly whipped cream,
Crema pasticcera (page 16) or diplomat cream (half pastry cream, half whipped
cream) before dusting with icing sugar.

Torta *di* Nonno Mario

NONNO MARIO'S CAKE

Serves 8–10

butter, for greasing

SPONGE
120 g (4½ oz) plain (all-purpose)
   flour (see note)
30 g (1 oz/¼ cup) cornflour
   (cornstarch) or potato starch
   (see note on page 25)
4 eggs, at room temperature
120 g (4½ oz) sugar

SYRUP
80 ml (2½ fl oz/⅓ cup) water
2 tablespoons Alchermes
   (see note and page 8) or rum
30 g (1 oz) sugar
rind of 1 lemon (optional)

PASTRY CREAMS
500 ml (17 fl oz/2 cups) full-cream
   (whole) milk
4 egg yolks
120 g (4½ oz) sugar
30 g (1 oz/¼ cup) cornflour
   (cornstarch)
1 vanilla bean, split lengthways and
   seeds scraped, or zest of 1 lemon
60 g (2 oz) dark chocolate, chopped

This is a cake for family celebrations – in our family, it's the cake that my husband's grandfather Nonno Mario would always make for birthdays, holidays and other special occasions, only substituting it in the summer for its chilled cousin, *Zuppa inglese* (page 146), which has basically all the same elements other than the sponge. Mario's wife, Lina, called it 'gattò' (gateau); my mother-in-law Angela calls it '*la torta traballosa*', 'wobbly cake', because Mario would put it together with warm pastry cream between the layers, which were not evenly sliced so it would lean and totter a little. There is a very similar dessert in the central Italian region of Abruzzo known as *pizza dolce*, and Italian-Americans would recognise it as 'Italian rum cake', while Italian-Australians call it 'continental cake'. But for us, it's simply 'Nonno Mario's cake'.

Preheat the oven to 180°C (350°F) and grease and line a 22 cm (8¾ in) round cake tin.

To make the sponge, sift the flours together into a bowl. In a separate bowl, whisk the eggs and sugar together for about 10 minutes until very creamy, pale, thick and pillowy. Fold in the flours very gently and pour into the tin.

Bake for 35 minutes, or until golden brown and springy on top. A skewer inserted in the middle of the cake should come out clean. Remove from the tin and leave to cool completely (even better if you make it the night before and refrigerate it overnight) before slicing into three even discs about 2 cm (¾ in) thick.

To make the syrup, combine all the ingredients in a small saucepan and bring to the boil. Simmer for 5 minutes, then take off the heat and set aside until needed.

To make the pastry creams, heat the milk in a saucepan until steaming but not boiling. In a heatproof bowl, whisk the yolks and sugar until smooth. Add the cornflour, vanilla or lemon and then the milk, a little bit at first, then combining the rest. Place the bowl in a bain-marie

>>

>>

DECORATION

250 ml (8½ fl oz/1 cup) pouring (single/light) cream

1 tablespoon cornflour (cornstarch)

3 tablespoons icing (confectioners') sugar

100 g (3½ oz) slivered almonds (optional; see note)

(double boiler; see page 10) and whisk steadily until thickened, about 12–15 minutes (it will thicken quite suddenly, so pay close attention when you see it begin to change).

Divide between two bowls and, in one, stir through the dark chocolate until melted and smooth. Leave to cool completely.

Assemble the cake by placing the bottom disc of cake on a flat plate or cake stand. Brush generously with the syrup. Smooth over the chocolate pastry cream. Place the middle layer of sponge on top. Brush again with the syrup, then smooth over the plain pastry cream. Place the final layer of cake on top. If serving the cake the next day, wrap well in plastic wrap until needed.

The day you plan to serve it, prepare the whipped cream: in a bowl, whisk the cream, cornflour and sugar until you just arrive at firm peaks. Cover the sides and top of the cake with the cream. If you want to, decorate with some slivered almonds. Serve in thin slices.

Notes

If you would like to make this wheat-free, use the *Torta margherita* (page 25) recipe in place of this sponge.

Instead of Alchermes, you can use rum or brandy, or replace the syrup entirely with strong espresso. To make it without any alcohol or caffeine, simply omit and use the syrup on its own.

The sponge, or *pan di spagna*, syrup and pastry creams can all be made up to a few days in advance, and the cake is best when put together the day before you want to serve it; it makes it a little more stable and less '*traballosa*'. Although Mario didn't decorate his cake with anything other than whipped cream, you could add crushed nuts, shaved chocolate or some fresh berries. Sometimes, instead of the whipped cream, Mario would cover the cake with warm, liquid chocolate that would drip down the sides.

Torta *di* pera *e* cioccolato

PEAR AND CHOCOLATE CAKE

This is a rich, elegant dessert inspired by one from a favourite Florentine pastry shop. Sometimes you can find this cake encased in a shortcrust pastry too, but I love this on its own, particularly when it has a dense melt-in-the-mouth texture like this one. The chocolate part of this cake is modelled on one of my own favourites: a flourless chocolate cake of Elizabeth David's.

Serves 8

50 g (1¾ oz) sugar
2 pears, peeled, cored and cut
    into eighths lengthways
150 g (5½ oz) dark chocolate
90 g (3 oz) unsalted butter, cubed
90 g (3 oz) caster (superfine) sugar
90 g (3 oz) almond meal
3 eggs, separated
1 teaspoon unsweetened cocoa
    powder, for dusting
icing (confectioners') sugar,
    for dusting (optional)

Combine the sugar with 500 ml (17 fl oz/2 cups) water in a saucepan and set over a medium heat. Add the pear and poach for 10–15 minutes, or until tender but not too soft (a knife should easily penetrate the flesh without any resistance). Drain and let the pear pieces cool.

Melt the chocolate over a bain-marie (double boiler; see page 10). When melted, remove from the heat, add the butter and stir until the butter has melted. Add the sugar and almond meal, stirring to combine. When the mixture is cool, add the egg yolks.

Preheat the oven to 180°C (350°F). Grease a 22–24 cm (8¾–9¼ in) round springform cake tin and dust with the cocoa powder.

In a separate bowl, whisk the egg whites to firm peaks, then fold them into the chocolate batter. Pour the chocolate mixture into the tin. Arrange the pear pieces on the top of the batter, pushing them slightly in. Bake for 40 minutes, or until a skewer inserted into the middle of the cake comes out clean.

When cool, remove the cake from the tin and, just before serving, dust liberally with icing sugar, if desired. Serve in modest slices – this is rather rich.

Tronco *al* cioccolato

CHOCOLATE-FILLED
SPONGE ROLL

Serves 6

2 tablespoons caster
    (superfine) sugar
125 ml (4 fl oz/½ cup) Alchermes
    (see note and page 8)
icing (confectioners') sugar,
    for dusting

CHOCOLATE PASTRY CREAM
100 g (3½ oz/⅔ cup) dark chocolate
    (70% cocoa)
2 egg yolks
60 g (2 oz) caster (superfine) sugar
1 tablespoon cornflour
    (corn starch), sifted
250 ml (8½ fl oz/1 cup) warm milk

SPONGE
50 g (1¾ oz) cornflour
    (corn starch) or potato starch
    (see note, page 25)
50 g (1¾ oz/⅓ cup) plain
    (all-purpose) flour
3 eggs, separated
100 g (3½ oz) caster (superfine)
    sugar

Tronco is a popular cake found all along the Tuscan coast. It literally means 'log' or 'trunk', and is almost always stained pink with Alchermes and filled with a rich chocolate cream or even chocolate-hazelnut spread. I find the latter too sweet and rich, and prefer it with a dark chocolate pastry cream.

The *pan di spagna*, or sponge, recipe, one of my favourites, is slightly adapted from my friend Emma Gardner's recipe – she is much more technical than me in the pastry department and I have simplified it somewhat, but it's the recipe I use most. I even make this *tronco* for Christmas. I double the recipe for two rolls and turn them into a yule log, decorating with a thick, chocolate icing, crumbled meringue for snow and candied rosemary.

For the pastry cream, melt the dark chocolate either in a microwave or over a bain-marie (double boiler; see page 10).

Use an electric mixer to whisk the yolks and sugar together until pale. Stir in the cornflour. Put the mixture in a saucepan over a low heat and slowly add the milk, little by little. (If your lowest burner is still quite aggressive, do this over a bain-marie (double boiler) so the eggs don't curdle from being heated too rapidly.) Stir continuously with a wooden spoon or silicone spatula until the mixture becomes smooth and thick and coats the back of a spoon, about 10 minutes (see note). Remove from the heat and stir through the melted chocolate. When it is smooth and well combined, cool quickly by spreading the pastry cream out into a shallow, flat container such as a glass lasagne dish or baking tray. Place the plastic wrap right over the top of the pastry cream, so the entire surface is in contact with the plastic wrap. This will ensure the pastry cream doesn't develop a skin. Keep in the fridge until needed.

Preheat the oven to 160°C (320°F) and line a 23 × 33 cm (9 × 13 in) baking tray with baking paper.

To make the sponge, sift the cornflour and flour together. Put the separated eggs in two clean metal or glass mixing bowls, yolks in one and whites in the other. Whisk the egg yolks and the sugar with an electric mixer or electric beaters for up to 10 minutes, or until

>>

the yolks become very pale and creamy. Clean the beaters very well, then whisk the whites until stiff peaks form. To the creamy egg yolks, gently fold in half of the whites and then half of the flours, and repeat with the remaining whites and flours until they are all combined.

Pour the batter into the lined baking tray – the batter should be about 1 cm (½ in) high. (You can also use a flat tray and spread the batter out to the size you like with a palette knife.) Bake in the oven for about 10–12 minutes, or until the top is very pale golden and the sponge is springy in the middle.

Remove the sponge from the oven and let it cool ever so slightly so you can handle it easily – you still want to work with it while it's warm. Spread out a sheet of plastic wrap and scatter it evenly with the caster sugar (this helps to stop the sponge from sticking to the plastic). Gently turn the sponge upside down onto the plastic wrap. Remove the baking paper to reveal a spongy soft cake. With a bread knife, trim the edges – this will stop the sides from cracking as they roll. Then, with a pastry brush, stain this side of the sponge evenly with Alchermes (see note). You may have to do a couple of 'coats' for a bright pink. Take the cooled pastry cream out of the fridge and generously spread it over the top of the pink sponge so that it is about 1.5 cm (½ in) thick, smoothing it out evenly and leaving a 1 cm (½ in) border around the edges.

The rolling part is rather like rolling sushi, if you've done it. The tricky part is really in starting the roll – the rest is all about the right amount of pressure (not too tight, but not too loose). Picking up the short end of the sponge with the help of the plastic wrap, carefully roll the entire thing up firmly and then secure by wrapping completely in the plastic wrap. Keep in the fridge to chill for 1 hour or overnight.

Remove the plastic wrap carefully, dust the top with icing sugar and serve in thick slices.

Notes

If at any point you start to see lumps appearing in the pastry cream, remove the pan from the heat and stir vigorously. You can also strain out the lumps using a fine-mesh sieve.

If you don't have Alchermes, you can make a rum (or other liqueur) syrup by bringing 125 ml (4 fl oz/½ cup) water and 125 g (4½ oz) sugar to a boil. Turn down to low and let simmer for 10 minutes, remove from the heat and add 2 tablespoons of rum. This is rather nice with a twist of orange peel added to the boiling syrup, too. For a non-boozy version, leave out the rum and just use the simple syrup to add moisture to the sponge – this will help it take and hold shape.

Torta *di* semolino *e* cioccolato

SEMOLINA AND CHOCOLATE TART

This tart is commonly found in Florentine pastry shops as a beautiful, whole tart with a topping of bittersweet, shiny ganache covering a filling of smooth semolina – a dessert fit to bring to a dinner party or for a special occasion. Semolina or durum wheat flour is a coarse, pale yellow flour used for making couscous and fresh pasta (particularly in egg-less pasta doughs). While semolina used for pasta can be quite coarse in texture, there's also a finer semolina flour that is used for baking bread in southern Italy. Here, fine semolina is cooked with milk until it becomes soft and creamy, much like polenta. When set, it has a pudding-like texture and is the perfect foil to the dark, rich ganache.

You only need about half of the Sweet shortcrust pastry recipe for this tart. You can halve the recipe (as indicated in the ingredients) or do what I do: make the whole amount and freeze what you don't use for making mini tarts or even simple cut-out cookies later.

Serves 8

½ quantity Sweet shortcrust
    pastry dough (see page 23)

SEMOLINA FILLING
500 ml (17 fl oz/2 cups) milk
pinch of salt
85 g (3 oz/⅔ cup) fine semolina
75 g (2¾ oz/⅓ cup) sugar
finely grated zest of 1 lemon
1 egg, beaten

CHOCOLATE GANACHE
75 ml (2½ fl oz) thick
    (double/heavy) cream
150 g (5½ oz) dark chocolate
    (70% cocoa), finely chopped

Preheat the oven to 180°C (350°F).

After resting the pastry dough, roll it out to a thickness of about 3–4 mm (about ⅛ in) and press into a 23 cm (9 in) pie dish, trimming the edges. Place a sheet of baking paper over the pastry and fill with baking beads (you can also use dried beans or uncooked rice that you can keep and re-use specifically for this purpose). Blind bake for 15 minutes.

Take the pastry out of the oven and remove the baking paper with the beads. Let the pastry cool.

Prepare the semolina by bringing the milk to the boil with the salt. Turn the heat to low–medium, add the semolina and whisk continuously until the mixture thickens to a thick porridge (oatmeal) consistency. This should take 8–10 minutes. Taste to check if it's ready – the semolina should feel soft in your mouth, not grainy. When ready, remove from the heat and stir in the sugar and zest until combined. When the mixture has cooled, stir in the egg. Spread the semolina mixture into the tart crust.

>>

>>   Bake at 180°C (350°F) for 40–45 minutes, or until the pastry is golden and the semolina feels firm and springy to the touch. Let it cool completely.

Prepare the ganache by bringing the cream to the boil in a small saucepan. Take off the heat, add the chocolate to the cream and stir or whisk until very smooth (see note). Pour the warm ganache over the cooled semolina tart and let it cool completely to set before slicing and serving.

Store in an airtight container in the fridge for up to 3 days.

Note

If the ganache separates, becoming lumpy and greasy, add a little dash of hot cream (or even hot water) until it is smooth.

Cavallucci

SPICED WALNUT BISCUITS

Cavallucci are spiced biscuits from Siena that, along with almond-studded *cantuccini* and soft, almond meal *ricciarelli*, are often served at the end of a special meal, in particular at Christmas. No one remembers exactly why these Renaissance-aged biscuits are named after 'little horses', but one theory is that they were traditionally served to the servants who worked in the stables that the city housed for their beloved horses (Siena is the city of the Palio, the world famous horse race, after all); another is that they were served in the countryside inns surrounding the city of Siena to passersby on horseback. Most convincing to me is the theory that they were a popular snack for Renaissance travellers passing through town on the Pilgrim route – the biscuits, made with honey (now usually with sugar syrup), nuts and spices, supplied weary travellers on horseback with energy and kept well on long trips.

Cavallucci are still traditionally eaten around Christmas time and are often given as gifts when visiting friends or family. Serve these as you would any Tuscan biscuit, with wine to dunk them in – in particular, dessert wine.

Makes 14 biscuits

300 g (10½ oz/1⅓ cups) sugar
1 tablespoon honey
100 g (3½ oz/1 cup) freshly shelled walnuts, finely chopped
50 (1¾ oz) candied orange rind, finely chopped
2 tablespoons aniseed, whole
2 teaspoons ground cinnamon
300 g (10½ oz/2 cups) plain (all-purpose) flour, plus extra for dusting

Preheat the oven to 170°C (340°F).

Prepare a syrup by dissolving the sugar in 100 ml (3½ fl oz) water in a small saucepan over a low heat. Simmer for about 5 minutes, until it reduces very slightly but – importantly – does not colour. Take it off the heat and mix in the honey, walnuts, candied orange and spices.

In a separate bowl, sift the flour. Add the hot syrup and mix together to form a dough. On a surface well-dusted with flour, roll apricot-sized balls of dough. Keeping them coated in flour makes them easier to handle. Place the balls on a baking tray lined with baking paper and pat to flatten them ever so slightly. Bake for 15–20 minutes, or until the cavallucci are hard to the touch but still pale. They should be soft and chewy inside (see note).

For celebrations

Note

Cavallucci should have a hard shell (the syrup helps this) but a soft interior, so do not bake them for too long. If you prefer a crunchier cookie, you can bake them a little longer, but try not to let them colour too much.

Variations

The syrup really takes the place of honey, which was used in centuries-old versions of *cavallucci*; feel free to substitute entirely with honey but beware that honey is sweeter than sugar so you can use less.

You can substitute fennel seeds for the aniseed, if you don't have it, or use any combination of the following ground spices in addition to or instead of the cinnamon: ground cloves, nutmeg, coriander seed.

Cenci

SWEET DEEP-FRIED PASTRY

Makes about 25 cenci

240 g (8½ oz) plain (all-purpose)
  flour
1 tablespoon caster (superfine)
  sugar
pinch of salt
1½ tablespoons olive oil, plus extra
  for deep-frying (see note)
2 eggs, beaten
1 tablespoon Alchermes
  (see note and page 8)
zest of 1 lemon
icing (confectioners') sugar,
  for dusting

Notes

Traditionally these are fried in lard, which is an excellent medium for frying for its non-greasy results (despite what many mistakenly think). A not-so-fruity olive oil is the next best choice, but try to avoid using peanut oil.

Alchermes, a centuries-old Florentine liqueur, lends the pastry a slightly spiced perfume but you could substitute rum or vin santo or, as Artusi does, even grappa.

Cenci means 'rags', which describes the crimp-edged, twisted shapes of this deep-fried pastry that appears in Florentine bakery shop windows and fairs during the wintery month of *Carnevale* (Carnival). Many Tuscans get that nostalgic look in their eye when they eat *cenci*, as it's a reminder of dressing up in masks and costumes as a child and biting into these warm, crunchy pastries.

Sift the flour, sugar and salt into a bowl. Make a well in the centre and add the 1½ tablespoons of oil, and the eggs, Alchermes and lemon zest and beat with a fork, starting from the centre and moving out to incorporate the flour. Finish with your hands to make a compact ball of dough. Wrap the dough in plastic wrap and let it rest for at least 30 minutes.

Roll out the dough on a lightly floured work surface to a 2–3 mm (⅛ in) thickness. With a frilled-edge pastry cutter, cut strips of dough about 2.5 cm (1 in) wide and 10 cm (4 in) long.

Heat enough oil in a saucepan so that the dough will float. If you have a sugar thermometer, use it to determine when the oil reaches 150°C (300°F). The dough needs to fry evenly, not too fast and not too slow. You can test with small pieces of leftover pastry dough – the oil is ready to use when the oil starts to bubble immediately, surrounding the dough entirely with tiny bubbles.

Deep-fry the cenci in batches, twisting them or knotting them as you drop them carefully in the hot oil. Cook for about 20–30 seconds per side until a golden-caramel colour. Remove with a slotted spoon and leave to drain on paper towel. They should not be oily or greasy at all, but crisp and dry. Dust with plenty of icing sugar while hot and serve warm or cold with a small glass of vin santo.

These are best eaten the day they are made.

Sfratti

HONEY AND NUT PASTRIES

There are still a handful of bakeries and little shops in the historic southern Tuscan town of Pitigliano that sell these hardy rolls of pastry filled with walnuts and honey, along with cinnamon-scented *Tozzetti Ebraici* (page 98). These delicious pastries are the town's most famous gastronomic tradition, and have survived despite their origins in the Jewish community, which no longer exists in Pitigliano.

The pastry's name comes from the Italian word for 'evicted', *sfratto*, and it is no coincidence that their stick-like appearance matches that of the batons once used by authorities attempting to evict Jews from their community.

Edda Servi Machlin writes, 'Much of Jewish food lore is based on reproducing, in a sweet form, some symbolic item of unhappy events of the past as a reminder of the constant and dreadful danger of their recurrence and also to ward off such a possibility.' Almost like a good luck charm. In fact, even the non-Jewish Pitiglianesi adopted this idea, and *sfratti* became a must-have to serve at weddings and other special occasions, for good fortune.

This recipe is adapted from Edda Servi Machlin's in *The Classic Cuisine of the Italian Jews* (1981). Sometimes you'll find the pastry made like a shortcrust pastry, which would be crumblier and softer, and some like to brush the *sfratti* with beaten egg yolk for a shiny glaze. But I like this one of Edda's, which is hard (almost brittle), but thin and so basic. It is more like the ones I've tried from Pitigliano.

For the pastry, combine the flour, sugar and salt in a bowl and make a well in the centre. Add the wine and the oil into the well and whisk the mixture together with a fork, moving from the centre outwards, gradually incorporating more dry ingredients. You want a smooth but quite firm dough. Knead for a few minutes, then roll into a disc shape (with a flattened top), cover in plastic wrap and set aside to rest for 30 minutes.

To make the filling, melt the honey in a saucepan over a high heat (watch carefully that it doesn't bubble over). Add the spices, orange zest and nuts, and cook for 3 minutes. Remove the saucepan from the heat and add the breadcrumbs, then transfer to a bowl to let it cool, turning occasionally to speed up the cooling process –

Makes 6 sfratti

PASTRY
350 g (12½ oz/2⅓ cups) plain (all-purpose) flour
150 g (5½ oz) sugar
pinch of salt
125 ml (4 fl oz/½ cup) dry white wine
80 ml (2½ fl oz/⅓ cup) olive oil

FILLING
350 g (12½ oz/1 cup) honey
½ teaspoon ground cinnamon
¼ teaspoon ground cloves
¼ teaspoon ground black pepper
¼ teaspoon ground nutmeg
finely grated zest of 1 orange
350 g (12½ oz) shelled walnuts, chopped very finely
2 tablespoons fine breadcrumbs

>> it will be very thick and sticky. When cool enough to handle, divide the honey and nut mixture into six portions. I find a knife works best for this. With wet hands, shape the filling into logs about 2.5 cm (1 in) thick.

Preheat the oven to 190°C (375°F) and line a baking tray with baking paper.

Divide the dough into six portions. With a rolling pin, roll out strips about 10 × 25 cm (4 × 10 in). Put a honey and nut log in the middle of the strip (make sure there is a little space for both ends of the 'log' to be sealed) and wrap the dough around it, overlapping slightly, to cover all the filling completely. Roll the entire pastry with both hands to seal and even out the dough, then place on the baking tray, seal side down. Press down on the ends to seal and tuck the extra pastry underneath.

Continue with the rest of the dough and filling.

Bake in the oven for 20 minutes, or until the dough is still quite pale but dry to the touch. Let it cool completely.

Wrap the cooled sfratti in aluminium foil; they keep well like this for weeks without refrigeration (as there are no eggs or dairy in this recipe). If you can wait, they taste better a day or two later. Cut into 1 cm (½ in) thick rounds and serve with coffee, but more traditional would be with a glass of vin santo or other dessert wine.

Frittelle
di riso

RICE FRITTERS

They like to say in Tuscany, '*Fritta è bona anche una ciabatta*' (even a slipper is good deep-fried).

These *frittelle di riso*, which are essentially deep-fried blobs of rice pudding, can be found in Florentine bakeries and food vans parked at fairs in February for *Carnevale* (Carnival), but are perhaps even more commonly associated with *la Festa del Papà* on March 19, Italian Father's Day and St Joseph's Day. It's fitting — aside from being the exemplar father, Joseph is also the patron saint of friers.

Like anything deep-fried, these fritters are best eaten when still hot and crisp. Once cold they turn soggy and the sugar melts away, so cook a batch of these when you plan to eat them right away.

Makes 25–30 fritters

100 g (3½ oz) short-grain risotto
     rice, such as arborio or carnaroli
     (see note)
500 ml (17 fl oz/2 cups) milk
2 eggs, beaten
1 tablespoon unsalted butter, melted
40 g (1½ oz) plain (all-purpose) flour
1 teaspoon baking powder
pinch of salt
zest of 1 lemon
zest of 1 orange
1 teaspoon natural vanilla extract
125 g (4½ oz) sugar
vegetable oil, for frying

Note

It's important to use starchy rice in this recipe, such as one that you would use for risotto. The starch released from the risotto rice ensures a softer, creamier filling than other types of rice.

Cook the rice and the milk in a saucepan over a low–medium heat, stirring frequently until the rice is soft and the mixture is thick and creamy, about 20 minutes (keep a careful eye on it so it doesn't overflow or burn).

Remove from the heat and let the rice cool slightly before mixing in the eggs, butter, flour, baking powder, salt, the citrus zest, vanilla and 1 tablespoon of the sugar.

Leave to cool completely and rest the mixture for several hours or, better, cool overnight in the fridge. The mixture should be a little bit runny, similar to pancake batter.

Pour enough oil in a saucepan so that the fritters will be able to float, and heat the oil to about 160° (320°F). Drop a small cube of bread in the oil to test whether it's ready — if the bread turns golden in 15 seconds, the oil is hot enough. Drop heaped teaspoon–sized blobs of mixture (measure it onto 1 teaspoon, then use another to push each fritter off the spoon) into the boiling oil. Deep-fry in batches of three or four for 2 minutes on each side (turning them over once), or until evenly deep golden brown.

When cooked, drain the fritters on paper towel for a moment, then roll them in the remaining sugar while still hot. Serve immediately. These are best eaten straight away.

Pagnottella

FIG AND CHOCOLATE BREAD

This wonderful specialty of Porto Santo Stefano on Monte Argentario in Tuscany's south coast is halfway between a fruit cake and something dense and chocolatey, like brownies. It's the kind of thing that you can't find in shops or restaurants or even in cookbooks – it's made at home by those who know the tradition best: nonnas.

I asked a few friends from Porto Santo Stefano if they had a good recipe for *pagnottella* that I could try and they all came back to me with cherished, handwritten family recipes from their mother or nonna, each of them slightly different. Alessandra's nonna makes this with some grated apple for moisture and keeps the chocolate in huge square inch–sized cubes, resulting in decadent pockets of melted chocolate like molten lava. Orestina makes a version with bread dough and insists on using home-made plum jam (very typical of Argentario, she notes). Valeria's mother, Filomena, cooks dried figs in vermouth for her *pagnottella*, which otherwise is very similar to Alessandra's nonna's. The one thing most recipes have in common is that the amount of flour called for is *quanto basta*, or as much as is needed. This means enough to bring the sticky mixture together into a soft dough.

This recipe is inspired mostly by Alessandra's nonna's recipe. It's quite soft, decadent and fruity – not to mention chocolatey. You only need a very thin slice of this, served with some dessert wine. It's traditionally made around Christmas time (these flavours and scents are particularly loved at this time of year) and, much like panforte or fruit cake, would make a nice gift for friends and family.

Pagnottella is either made as one large loaf or a few buns, dusted in flour before being baked to set. A variation is to mix all the ingredients into bread dough instead of just flour so that you have a rather hard, dense fruit and nut loaf. All versions keep a very long time and just get better as they age.

>>

>>

Serves 12

250 g (9 oz/1⅔ cups) dried figs,
    roughly chopped
500 ml (17 fl oz/2 cups) white wine
¼ apple, peeled, cored and grated
100 g (3½ oz) dark chocolate
    (70% cocoa), chopped roughly
zest of 1 orange
50 g (1¾ oz) sultanas (golden raisins)
50 g (1¾ oz/⅓ cup) pine nuts
50 g (1¾ oz/½ cup) walnut kernels
50 g (1¾ oz/⅓ cup) whole almonds
50 g (1¾ oz) whole hazelnuts, peeled
2 tablespoons unsweetened
    cocoa powder
2 tablespoons plum jam
¼ teaspoon ground cinnamon
¼ teaspoon ground nutmeg
100 g (3½ oz/⅔cup) plain
    (all-purpose) flour or as
    needed, plus extra for
    dusting (see note)

Soak the figs in the wine overnight. Put the soaked figs with all the liquid in a small saucepan and add the grated apple. Bring to a simmer and cook over a low–medium heat until the fruit is soft and the liquid has reduced slightly, about 15 minutes. Blend in a food processor or with a hand-held blender until paste-like. Let it cool.

Transfer the fig mixture to a large bowl and add the rest of the ingredients except for the flour and combine. Add the flour in a few stages until you have a soft and sticky mixture that has the consistency of bread dough – you may need to add a bit more or a bit less.

Preheat the oven to 160°C (320°F), line a baking tray with baking paper and dust the top with flour.

Directly on the baking tray, use floured hands to shape the dough into a round loaf about 20 cm (8 in) wide and flatten it until it's about 5 cm (2 in) tall in the centre. Dust liberally with flour on the top and blow off the excess. Bake in the oven for 25–30 minutes, or until the flour on the tray turns a cappuccino-coloured brown and the bread feels firm.

This delicious bread lasts ages and ages and ages. It's best to keep it covered/wrapped in plastic wrap or in an airtight container, and stored somewhere cool and dry.

Note

I find 100 g (3½ oz) of flour is enough, but all flours are different, and all figs will likely be different too, so use this as a guideline. You might find that your dough can take a lot more.

Variations

If you don't have plum jam, you can use another dark jam such as grape or fig, or even substitute completely with honey. I like this even mixture of different nuts, but you could cut it down to one or two kinds. Just choose 200 g (7 oz) of any nuts – my friend Orestina likes to use just almonds, for example. You can also use red wine for cooking the figs. Sometimes you'll see this bread in a stick shape – a long loaf rather than a round one.

Bonet Chocolate and amaretti flan/ *Zuccotto* Ricotta and chocolate filled sponge cake/ *Budino di riso* Baked rice pudding/ *Sanguinaccio al cioccolato* Chocolate pudding/ *Zuppa inglese*/ *Ricotta al caffe* Coffee-laced ricotta/ *Zabaione*/ *Latte alla Portoghese* Tuscan baked custard

Dolci *al* cucchiaio/

To eat with a spoon

Soft and creamy treats, from trifle-like
zuppa inglese to chocolate pudding and
baked custard.

Bonet

CHOCOLATE AND
AMARETTI FLAN

This centuries-old dessert from Piedmont is a bit like crème caramel, but flavoured with chocolate and amaretti biscuits. It needs nothing more than the bittersweet caramel spooned over the top, but you could decorate it with whipped cream, some whole or crushed amaretti, or a sprinkling of finely chopped hazelnuts.

Like other classic Piedmont desserts, such as *Stuffed peaches* (page 68), this is usually made with the crunchy *amaretti di Saronno*, not the softer *amaretti di Sassello*, but if you have trouble finding them you can use Savoiardi (page 17) with a splash of amaretto liqueur for that special almond flavour.

Serves 6–8

butter, for greasing
175 g (6 oz) sugar
4 eggs
375 ml (12½ fl oz/1½ cups)
    full-cream (whole) milk,
    warmed
15 g (½ oz) unsweetened cocoa
    powder, sifted
35 g (1¼ oz) amaretti (about 10 small
    amaretti biscuits), crushed, plus
    extra for decoration
splash of rum, grappa or similar
    (optional)

Note

You could also prepare this in a
pudding mould or even in individual
ovenproof ramekins.

Lightly grease a loaf (bar) tin, approximately 11 × 25 cm (4¼ × 10 in) (see note), and preheat the oven to 150°C (300°F).

Place 100 g (3½ oz) of the sugar in a saucepan and shake or tap the pan so that the sugar sits in a flat layer. Add 1 tablespoon of water and melt gently over a low–medium heat. Slowly, the sugar will melt and bubble, appearing first to look crystallised. Resist any temptation to stir it, but keep an eye on it until the sugar begins to turn liquid and then a pale amber colour. Now it will begin to change quite quickly; you can give the pan a swirl to make sure all the sugar crystals melt. As soon as it is completely liquid and the sugar is a deep amber colour, remove from the heat and pour it into the tin. In total, this should take 5–7 minutes. Set the pan aside and let it cool.

In a mixing bowl, gently whisk the eggs and the rest of the sugar by hand. Slowly add the warm milk, along with the sifted cocoa powder. Strain the mixture into another bowl, then add the crushed amaretti and the rum, if using. Pour into the tin, over the top of the caramel, then place the tin in a large, deep baking dish. Pour hot water into the baking dish to come halfway up the side of the tin holding the bonet mixture and bake for 50 minutes, or until the top is set and springy.

Remove from the oven and leave to cool completely before chilling in the fridge for a few hours or overnight. To serve, run a thin, sharp knife around the edges of the bonet, then turn it out onto a long, flat plate. Serve in slices with the caramel spooned over the top.

To eat with a spoon

Zuccotto

RICOTTA AND CHOCOLATE
FILLED SPONGE CAKE

Some say this very Florentine dessert of Italian sponge, *pan di spagna*, encasing a sweet ricotta filling dates back to the sixteenth century and may have been created by multitasking Renaissance architect Bernardo Buontalenti, who the Florentines also like to credit as the inventor of gelato. To me what makes this so Florentine is its shape – the dome so reminiscent of the more famous dome atop the Duomo. When I see rows of these bright pink domes in pastry shop fridges, I can't help but think of the comparison, but actually the dessert probably gets its name from its similarity to the little red caps worn by priests, which are nicknamed *zuccotti*.

The pink liqueur that characteristically stains a zuccotto is Alchermes. A Tuscan liqueur that was once touted as an elixir for longevity and used to revive weary spirits, it's now only used in a number of traditional desserts for its colour.

Zuccotto is made in two different ways: it's either frozen and served as a semifreddo (rather like an ice-cream cake) or it's simply refrigerated and served fresh. With this recipe, you can do either and have good results, but I prefer the latter.

Serves 6–8

SPONGE
120 g (4½ oz) plain (all-purpose)
   flour (or potato starch;
   see note on page 25),
   plus extra for dusting
120 g (4½ oz) sugar
3 eggs

FILLING
500 g (1 lb 2 oz) fresh ricotta
75 g (2¾ oz) caster (superfine) sugar
200 ml (7 fl oz) thick (double/heavy)
   cream, whipped
50 g (1¾ oz) dark chocolate, finely
   chopped
30 g (1 oz) candied orange peel,
   finely chopped (see note)
30 g (1 oz/¼ cup) unsweetened
   cocoa powder

SYRUP
50 g (1¾ oz) sugar
65 ml (2¼ fl oz) Alchermes
   (see page 8)

For the sponge, preheat the oven to 160°C (320°F). Lightly grease a 22 cm (8¾ in) round cake tin and dust with flour.

In a metal bowl set over a bain-marie (double boiler; see page 10), beat the sugar and eggs together with electric beaters until the mixture reaches 45°C (110°F) and is doubled in size and pale, thick and creamy. This should take about 3 minutes. Fold in the flour, bit by bit, until smooth.

Pour the mixture into the tin. Bake for 20 minutes, or until golden brown and springy. Gently remove the cake from the tin and let it cool on a rack.

For the filling, beat the ricotta and sugar together until creamy. Fold the whipped cream through and divide the mixture evenly into two bowls. In one, combine the chopped chocolate and candied orange peel. In the other, add the cocoa powder and mix until thoroughly combined.

>> For the syrup, dissolve the sugar in 200 ml (7 fl oz) water in a small saucepan and bring to the boil. Take off the heat and add the Alchermes. Let cool.

To assemble the zuccotto, line a deep, medium-sized bowl with plastic wrap. A mixing bowl shape is ideal, about 18 cm (7 in) in diameter at the rim and 9 cm (3½ in) tall.

Slice the sponge into 1 cm (½ in) thick slices. Dip slices on the cut side, one by one, into the syrup and place a layer of the slices, with the dipped side facing down, side by side, until the bowl is completely covered. Brush the slices on the inside with some of the Alchermes syrup. Spoon on the ricotta cream, covering the bottom and sides evenly. Spoon the cocoa ricotta cream inside and smooth over the top. Place more sponge slices side by side over the top, trimming where necessary, and brush with the rest of the Alchermes syrup.

Cover with plastic wrap, place a plate on top with a weight (a couple of tins of tomatoes, for example) and refrigerate for at least 4 hours or overnight.

To serve, remove the plate and plastic wrap from the top of the bowl and flip the zuccotto onto a serving plate. Remove and discard all of the plastic wrap. Slice the zuccotto into wedges with a sharp knife.

If you want to serve this frozen, freeze the zuccotto instead of refrigerating and remove from the freezer 1 hour before serving.

Note
If you are not a fan of candied orange peel, try the fresh zest of an orange in its place.

Budino
di riso

BAKED RICE PUDDING

This delicious, rustic and homely baked rice pudding comes right out of Pellegrino Artusi's classic cookbook, with a few modifications. It is one of our family's favourite recipes. My mother-in-law, Angela, often serves it with warm, liquid chocolate (*Sanguinaccio al cioccolato*, page 145) spooned over the top. I can't help but think of it as bread and butter pudding made with rice instead; it tastes remarkably similar.

It is best eaten warm, when it has not long been out of the oven. It doesn't keep well for longer than a day or two, as the rice tends to harden. So, although it's usually made in one large baking dish, if you're serving fewer people, you can halve this quantity and bake it in individual ramekins.

Serves 8–10

160 g (5½ oz) short-grain risotto rice, such as arborio or carnaroli
750 ml (25½ fl oz/3 cups) full-cream (whole) milk, or as needed
pinch of salt
100 g (3½ oz) sugar
½ vanilla bean, split lengthways and seeds scraped
zest of 1 lemon
40 g (1½ oz) butter, plus extra for greasing
100 g (3½ oz) raisins
2 whole eggs, plus 2 egg yolks
splash of rum, Cognac or vin santo (optional)
1 tablespoon breadcrumbs

Combine the rice with the milk in a saucepan and bring to a simmer with the pinch of salt. After 10 minutes, add the sugar, vanilla seeds, lemon zest and butter, and continue cooking over a low–medium heat for 30 minutes, or until the rice is very soft and the milk is almost all absorbed. If you notice the rice is absorbing the milk too quickly, add more milk – up to another 250 ml (8½ fl oz/1 cup) – until the rice is cooked. Remove from the heat.

Preheat the oven to 180°C (350°F).

When the rice mixture has cooled slightly but is still hot, add the raisins, eggs, yolks and rum, and stir well.

Grease a solid 25 cm (10 in) round cake tin or similar-sized baking dish with butter and scatter over breadcrumbs to coat all sides. Pour the rice mixture into the tin or dish and bake for 20 minutes, or until the top is golden brown.

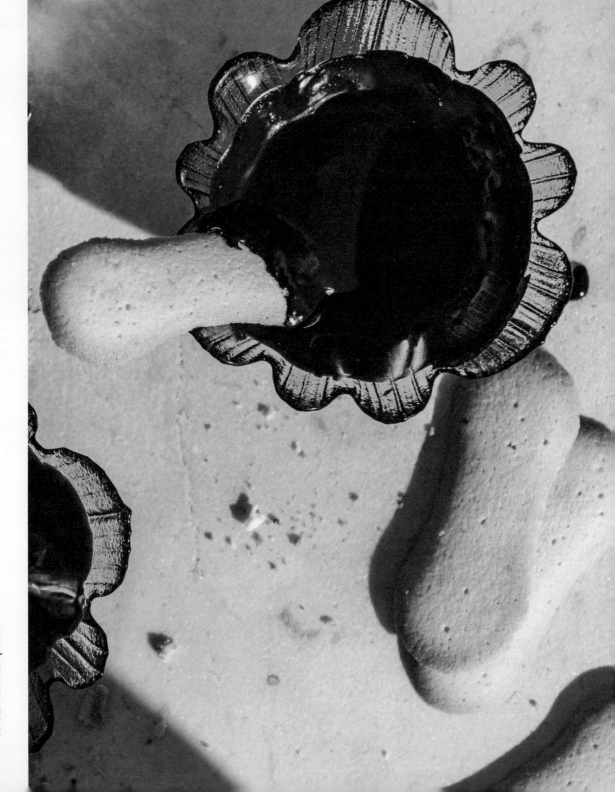

Sanguinaccio *al* cioccolato

CHOCOLATE PUDDING

My mother-in-law, Angela, often makes *dolce al cioccolato*, as she calls it, *ad occhio* (by eye) with just cocoa powder, flour, sugar and milk. It's rather like a very thick hot chocolate that she pours over the top of rice pudding and home-made celebration cakes.

Angela's handwritten notes on her mother, Lina's, recipe include flavouring the chocolate with vanilla and cinnamon, which are very typical of traditional *sanguinaccio*, an ancient, southern Italian specialty made with chocolate and pig blood. Some other optional flavours to add would be lemon or orange zest, or a splash of rum or your favourite liqueur. I like to add a bit of dark chocolate (the best quality I can find) to Lina's basic recipe, which adds depth and a silky, denser texture to the finished pudding.

This is lovely when eaten completely chilled with a bit of freshly whipped cream and some tart, fresh berries for dessert (making this a really easy dessert to prepare ahead of time, as it benefits from an overnight rest in the fridge). But it is equally good when eaten still warm with some simple biscotti or Savoiardi (page 17) for dipping as a decadent afternoon snack on a cold day, the way Nonna Lina would have served it.

Serves 6-8

200 g (7 oz) sugar
150 g (5½ oz) unsweetened cocoa powder
30 g (1 oz) plain (all-purpose) flour
600 ml (20½ fl oz) milk, warmed
70 g (2½ oz) dark chocolate (70% cocoa), roughly chopped

Combine the dry ingredients in a heavy-based saucepan. Add the warm milk, a little at a time, so that you create a thick but smooth paste out of the dry ingredients. Continue adding milk, stirring with a wooden spoon or whisk the whole time, until you have a smooth mixture. Place over a very low heat and bring the mixture to a simmer for about 10–15 minutes, stirring constantly. When it thickens enough to heavily coat the spoon (if you drag a spoon across the bottom of the pan, you should be able to see a line momentarily), remove from the heat.

At this point, you have yourself some lovely, thick, decadent hot chocolate, but to continue making puddings, stir through the dark chocolate until melted. Pour the mixture into individual serving bowls or ramekins, or even into one large bowl to serve at the table. Leave it to cool, then put it in the fridge to chill and finish setting completely (if serving with cream and berries, add these on top or on the side at the last moment), or eat it warm, as is, with biscuits.

Zuppa inglese

This Tuscan classic is a simple, sometimes gaudy, yet much-loved dessert made of layers of chocolate and plain pastry creams and pink, Alchermes-soaked Savoiardi (page 17).

The similarity to British trifle is so striking that the literal translation of its name, 'English soup', probably comes as no surprise and, indeed, many assume that zuppa inglese is an Italianised English trifle, brought over by English expatriates living in Florence in the nineteenth century.

But I'm quite positive that it is an age-old Italian preparation simply named in honour of the English, perhaps from the traditional use of *crema Inglese* (literally 'English cream', otherwise known as *crème anglaise* or pouring custard, which is made without any starch). In Pellegrino Artusi's 1891 recipe for zuppa inglese, he cites it as a Tuscan dessert, saying that the delicate *crema Inglese* that the Tuscans like to use is too runny for his liking so he uses *crema pasticcera*, pastry cream, thickened with starch, which is how it's usually made today.

The apricot jam is not common these days, but it is included in Artusi's recipe and I've always liked the contrasting tart flavour it gives and the colour it adds. If you want to make a non-alcoholic version, use the sugar syrup without the Alchermes and rum, or you can use coffee instead. If you don't have a deep glass bowl – at least 10 cm (4 in) deep and 22 cm (8¾ in) in diameter, but you can easily go a bit bigger – you can also use a large rectangular glass dish.

Serves 8–10

PASTRY CREAMS
8 egg yolks
170 g (6 oz/¾ cup) caster
   (superfine) sugar
80 g (2¾ oz) cornflour (cornstarch)
½ vanilla bean, split lengthways
   and seeds scraped
1 litre (34 fl oz/4 cups) full-cream
   (whole) milk, warmed
100 g (3½ oz) dark chocolate,
   finely chopped

TO ASSEMBLE
2 tablespoons sugar
50 ml (1¾ fl oz) rum
125 ml (4 fl oz/½ cup) Alchermes
   (see page 8)
400 g (14 oz) Savoiardi
   (page 17; see note)
100 g (3½ oz) apricot jam
   (see page 23)
250 ml (8½ fl oz/1 cup) single
   (pouring) cream, whipped,
   to serve
unsweetened cocoa powder,
   to serve (optional)

To eat with a spoon

To make the pastry creams, whisk the yolks and sugar until smooth in a heatproof bowl. Add the cornflour, vanilla seeds and then the milk, a little bit at first, then combining the rest. Place the bowl over a bain-marie (double boiler; see page 10) and whisk steadily until thickened, about 12–15 minutes (it will thicken quite suddenly, so pay close attention when you see it begin to change).

Set aside roughly two-thirds of the pastry cream in a shallow bowl to cool it quickly, giving it a stir every now and then so that a skin doesn't form (if making this well in advance, cover with plastic wrap that touches the top of the pastry cream and store in the fridge). Stir the chocolate into the rest of the still-hot pastry cream, mixing until smooth. Set aside to cool.

>> Prepare a syrup by dissolving the sugar in 125 ml (4 fl oz/½ cup) water in a small saucepan and allowing to simmer for about 5 minutes. Add the rum and Alchermes and continue simmering for another 5 minutes (if you like it boozy, let the syrup cool before stirring in the alcohol).

Dip the savoiardi on both sides into the Alchermes mixture and place the biscuits side by side to cover the bottom of a glass serving bowl.

Cover the savoiardi with a layer of apricot jam, then half of the plain pastry cream. Add another layer of Alchermes-dipped savoiardi, followed by a layer of the chocolate pastry cream, another layer of dipped savoiardi and the rest of the plain pastry cream.

If you have the space, you can add an extra layer of dipped savoiardi, then cover and chill in the fridge for at least 2 hours (or overnight) before topping with freshly whipped cream just before serving. Alternatively, leave off the top layer of savoiardi and chill the zuppa inglese as described. Before serving, dust with cocoa powder (if using) and serve with the cream on the side.

Note

This is often made with sponge cake cut into thin slices and then fingers – savoiardi are, after all, simply sponge cake made into dry biscuits. If you want to try the sponge, use the recipe for Nonno Mario's cake (page 111) or, if you want a wheat-free version, you can use the recipe for Torta margherita (page 25).

Ricotta *al* caffe

<u>COFFEE-LACED RICOTTA</u>

This is an incredibly simple dessert inspired by a lovely little recipe in Elizabeth David's 1954 cookbook, *Italian Food*. She suggests serving it with some fresh cream and thin wafer biscuits (I quite like *lingua di gatto*, or cat's tongue biscuits, for this). Together with the booziness from the rum and the uplifting hit of caffeine, it's rather like a lazy idea for a tiramisu.

I've made it many times since and it has morphed a little from the original. I prefer it with a shot of espresso rather than coffee grounds for a subtler coffee flavour. Sometimes I like to fold the whipped cream directly into the ricotta, which makes it light as a cloud. And, when I want to make it a little more substantial to serve as a dessert, I crumble biscuits into the glasses and layer them with the ricotta, whipped cream and chocolate. Served well chilled in little glasses, it is a refreshing, elegant and surprisingly light way to end a meal.

Serves 4

250 g (9 oz/1 cup) fresh ricotta
80 g (2¾ oz/⅓ cup) caster
    (superfine) sugar
2 tablespoons strong espresso
splash of rum (optional)
100 g (3½ oz) soft, plain biscuits
    (about 8), such as Savoiardi
    (page 17) or cat's tongue biscuits
100 ml (3½ fl oz) pouring (single/
    light) cream, whipped to soft
    peaks, to serve
20 g (¾ oz) dark chocolate,
    shaved or grated, to serve

Whip the ricotta with a whisk (if you prefer to remove all of the ricotta's characteristic lumps, you can make it perfectly smooth by passing it through a fine-mesh sieve with a silicone spatula to help you). Add the sugar, espresso and rum, if using, and whisk until smooth and well combined.

Crumble the biscuits and divide half of the crumble among the glasses. Distribute half of the ricotta mixture over the top. Add a layer of the remaining crumbled biscuits, then a layer of the rest of the ricotta mixture. Allow to chill for 1 hour before serving, then dollop whipped cream on the top and sprinkle with the dark chocolate.

Note

This dessert should sit for at least 1 hour in the fridge to chill before serving, but if you want to prepare this well ahead of time, such as the night before, leave off the whipped cream and shaved chocolate until just before serving.

To eat with a spoon

Zabaione

Pellegrino Artusi has a recipe called 'An egg for a child' in his 1891 cookbook, *Science in the Kitchen and the Art of Eating Well*. Like a warm, pillowy version of custard, it's nothing more than a fluffy, eggy cream, as simple and wholesome a snack as can be, made by whipping the white of an egg and folding it through the egg yolk with sugar. It is rather similar to this more traditional *zabaione* (pictured on page 104) — just leave out the egg white and add a splash of hot espresso (or rum, Marsala or vin santo) instead, which is what my husband, Marco, would get served as a child by his Nonna Lina for a boost of energy before soccer practice. Lina enjoyed serving coffee to anyone, especially young people! Today, Marco's favourite way of enjoying *zabaione* is with a splash of vin santo, a Tuscan dessert wine. Whatever you use, make sure it is good, as nothing is hidden in this simple preparation — and you can, of course, leave out both the alcohol or coffee, if you prefer.

Serves 1

1 very fresh organic free-range
   egg yolk
2 teaspoons caster (superfine) sugar
50 ml (1¾ fl oz) Marsala, vin santo
   or other young dessert wine
   (or hot espresso)

Prepare a bain-marie (double boiler; see page 10).

Whisk the yolk and sugar together in a small, heatproof bowl until the mixture becomes pale and creamy. Add the alcohol. Place the bowl over the bain-marie (double boiler) and continue whisking until the mixture is thick, creamy and fluffy. Take it off the heat just when you think it is almost ready — like many egg dishes, this is delicate and will continue to cook a little even after you take it off the heat.

Serve warm, alone, with a spoon, or with biscotti, such as the *Paste di meliga* (page 105) for dipping.

Latte *alla* Portoghese

TUSCAN BAKED CUSTARD

This is an old-fashioned Tuscan dessert, so old there are references to the Medici family's Portuguese guests being behind the name, and Artusi has a few versions of this crème caramel–like custard in his nineteenth-century cookbook. As the name will tell you (it translates literally to 'Portuguese-style milk'), this is made with just milk, no cream, which can be too heavy in these desserts. I like this simply flavoured with a split vanilla bean infused in the milk, but a thick piece of lemon peel is nice too. Artusi suggests coriander seed or coffee.

Serves 6

1 litre (34 fl oz/4 cups) full-cream (whole) milk
1 vanilla bean, split lengthways
170 g (6 oz/3/4 cup) sugar
2 whole eggs, plus 6 egg yolks

Note
It's usually baked in a ring-shaped pudding tin but use what you have, keeping in mind the larger the tin, the shorter this custard will be and therefore you may need to adjust the cooking time. I like it in an oval dish that has about a 1 litre (34 fl oz/4 cup) capacity and is about 23 cm (9 in) long and 16 cm (6¼ in) wide – the resulting dessert comes out nice and tall – but you could use a rectangular baking tray or a cake tin (not springform, as it would leak), even individual ramekins – really whatever you can easily fit inside another baking tray that will be filled with hot water for the bain-marie (double boiler).

Put the milk and vanilla bean in a saucepan over a medium heat. As soon as it is about to simmer, reduce the heat to low to ensure a gentle simmer. Watch it, as it will overflow suddenly if you aren't careful. Keep it at a gentle simmer for about 10 minutes, then remove from the heat and strain through a fine-mesh sieve into a jug.

Put 70 g (2½ oz/⅓ cup) of the sugar in a small saucepan and add 1 tablespoon of water. Bring to a simmer over a low heat and watch the syrup carefully until it turns amber. Remove from the heat and pour immediately into your heatproof dish or tin of choice (see note) to cover the bottom. Don't worry if the syrup solidifies. Set aside. Preheat the oven to 160°C (320°F).

By hand, whisk together the eggs, yolks and the remaining sugar in a bowl. Keep in mind you don't want the mixture to be too frothy.

When the milk has cooled to the temperature of a warm bath, add it a little at a time to the egg mixture until you have gently incorporated all of it. Pour over the top of the caramel.

Fill a larger baking tray with hot water and place the custard dish inside so that the water reaches halfway up the dish. Place in the oven.

Bake for 45 minutes, or until the custard is set and the top and edges are gently browned. Run a knife around the edge of the dish, place a serving plate (ideally one with a lip to catch the caramel) over the top and, with two hands, flip everything over in one swift, confident movement. Cut into slices and spoon over some extra caramel.

Semifreddo al cioccolato Chocolate semifreddo/ *Spumone* Ice-cream cake/ *Gelato al fior di latte* Milk gelato/ *Gelato di riso* Rice gelato/ *Sorbetto di susine* Plum sorbet/ *Granita al melone* Melon granita

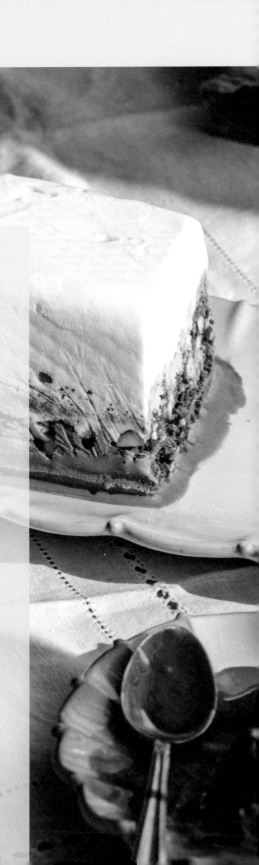

Dolci gelati/

Frozen treats

The perfect end after a big Italian dinner is a late night *passeggiata* (stroll) for a gelato or sorbetto. Here you'll find recipes for home-made gelato, refreshing granita and more frozen favourites.

Semifreddo *al* cioccolato

CHOCOLATE SEMIFREDDO

Semifreddo is a great way to make a frozen treat that has the creaminess of gelato but without the churning or any special equipment. It relies on an Italian meringue (which is made with hot sugar syrup that not only pasteurises the egg whites but, most importantly, keeps the fluffy meringue stable) for its texture, almost like a frozen mousse.

You can either pour this into a rectangular container to serve it in thick slices or you can freeze it in any airtight container and serve it in scoops like gelato.

Serves 4–6

75 g (2¾ oz/½ cup) dark chocolate
  (70% cocoa; see note), chopped
200 ml (7 fl oz) pouring (single/light)
  cream
1 egg white, room temperature
70 g (2½ oz/⅓ cup) sugar

Melt the chocolate and cream together in a metal bowl set over a bain-marie (double boiler; see page 10), stirring occasionally, until the chocolate has completely melted. Let the mixture cool, then chill in the fridge until needed. If you notice that the chocolate separates a little (this won't happen if you use a good quality chocolate, I find), you can whip it with electric beaters until it is perfectly smooth.

For the Italian meringue, whip the egg white in a clean, large bowl until soft and fluffy (see note). Set aside.

Make a sugar syrup by combining the sugar with 2 tablespoons of water in a saucepan over a low–medium heat. Let it simmer for a few minutes (if you have a sugar thermometer it should reach 120°C/250°F), then pour the hot syrup immediately down the side of the bowl into the egg whites while you continue whipping the mixture until the bowl feels cool to the touch and the mixture is very thick and glossy, and doesn't move if the bowl is tilted; this usually takes 7 minutes, but it can take anywhere between 5 and 10 minutes.

Fold the chilled chocolate mixture gently through the meringue until combined.

If you want to serve in slices, put the mixture in a rectangular container such as a loaf (bar) tin (you can line it with muslin or plastic wrap to make it easy to remove) and freeze until very firm, overnight ideally. Otherwise, for scooping, pour the mixture into any airtight container and freeze for at least 4 hours. If you have left it overnight, you may need to remove it from the freezer about 10 minutes before serving to let it soften slightly.

Notes

Use the best chocolate you can for this and you will be rewarded with a delicious, smooth, chocolately semifreddo. I personally like to use 70% cocoa Lindt chocolate. If you use a sweeter chocolate I would suggest reducing the sugar slightly or this might be on the sweet side.

Be careful not to whip the egg whites too stiffly – they should be soft and fluffy, not whipped to stiff peaks, otherwise the resulting semifreddo can have a crumbly rather than creamy texture.

Variations

Chocolate semifreddo is such a classic you don't need to do much else to it, but you could try it with a handful of chopped toasted hazelnuts mixed through for crunch, or some mint leaves infused in the cream (and then removed). If you like, decorate with some whipped cream and extra chocolate, grated or chopped, over the top.

Spumone

ICE-CREAM CAKE

A classic southern Italian dessert, *spumone* is a simple dome or loaf-shaped ice-cream cake, served sliced into wedges, revealing two tones of gelato (perhaps hazelnut and chocolate) and a heart of boozy sponge or Savoiardi (page 17). Sometimes candied or praline almonds or almond brittle – a treat known as *cupeta* in Puglia, in Italy's south – are crushed and mixed through the softened gelato or feature as a layer themselves.

Home-made *spumone* is a treat at any time, and this recipe is a breeze whether made from scratch with the help of an ice-cream machine or with your favourite store-bought gelato. In either case, you just need to start making it a little ahead of time so that you give each component enough time to chill. I've opted for fior di latte (milk) and chocolate gelato – family favourites – with an inner layer of savoiardi dipped in coffee (you can use milk for kids or add a splash of rum if it's for adults only) and crushed almond brittle. If making it with store-bought gelato, you'll need to remember to take the gelato out of the freezer to soften slightly before spreading into layers.

For the gelati, heat the milk and sugar in a saucepan until it is almost boiling (but watch it carefully; you mustn't let it boil). You should find the sugar has dissolved and the surface of the milk is frothy. Remove from the heat and pour half of the milk into a container. Leave it to cool completely.

To the milk left in the saucepan (while it is still hot), add the chocolate and cocoa and whisk until smooth. Let it cool, then chill it in the fridge.

Once the milk and sugar has cooled, add the cream and chill it in the fridge.

Churn the fior di latte (milk) gelato in an ice-cream machine according to the manufacturer's instructions. You may need to clean and let the ice-cream machine re-freeze in the freezer before doing the chocolate gelato, but check the instructions.

Serves 6–8

50 g (1¾ oz) Savoiardi (page 17)
60 ml (2 fl oz/¼ cup) espresso coffee (or milk), cooled

GELATI

1 litre (34 fl oz/4 cups) full-cream (whole) milk
200 g (7 oz) sugar
100 g (3½ oz) dark chocolate (70% cocoa), roughly chopped
30 g (1 oz/¼ cup) unsweetened cocoa powder
250 ml (8½ fl oz/1 cup) pouring (single/light) cream

CUPETA

100 g (3½ oz/⅔ cup) whole, raw almonds
60 g (2 oz) sugar

>>

While the gelato is still soft, pour it into a loaf (bar) tin lined with plastic wrap and smooth it out with a spatula. Cover with plastic wrap and place it in the freezer to harden for a few hours or overnight.

Churn the chocolate gelato in the ice-cream machine until soft and creamy.

Meanwhile, make the cupeta. Place the almonds, sugar and 1 tablespoon of water in a single layer in the bottom of a frying pan set over a medium heat. Cook until the sugar begins to melt and turn caramel brown. Shake the pan occasionally as the sugar melts, then toss the almonds with the caramel until toasted and well coated. Altogether, this process may only take about 5 minutes. Pour the mixture onto a baking tray or chopping board lined with baking paper and leave to cool. Before it is completely cool and hardened, chop finely with a heavy knife.

Dip the savoiardi into the coffee (or milk) and place a layer of them evenly over the fior di latte gelato in the loaf tin. Sprinkle over the chopped cupeta, then smooth over the softened, just-churned chocolate gelato right to the top.

Cover with plastic wrap and freeze until the chocolate gelato has hardened, preferably overnight. Turn out the spumone onto a flat serving plate, remove the plastic wrap and cut thick slices with the help of a large knife dipped in hot water.

Variations

Other than changing up the gelato flavours, you may like to use different nuts for the brittle, stir the crushed brittle into the gelato, or use chopped chocolate, candied fruit or anything else that takes your fancy.

Gelato *al* fior *di* latte

MILK GELATO

Made from just three ingredients, *fior di latte* is as wholesome and simple as can be, with the full flavour of milk but without the richness of a custard-based gelato (known as *crema* in Italian) or ice cream. Perhaps that's what makes it a popular flavour with children and adults alike – it is our family's number-one favourite – and one that is never missing from any Italian *gelateria*.

Makes about 900 ml (30 fl oz) of gelato (6–8 serves)

500 ml (17 fl oz/2 cups) full-cream (whole) milk
150 g (5½ oz) sugar
250 ml (8½ fl oz/1 cup) pouring cream (single/light), chilled

Combine the milk and sugar together in a saucepan over a low–medium heat. It should not boil, but just reach the point where tiny bubbles appear around the edges of the pan. Take the pan off the heat.

Cover and allow to cool to room temperature. Add the cream and churn in an ice-cream machine according to the manufacturer's instructions until frozen and creamy but firm.

Serve immediately for a softer style gelato or put the mixture in an airtight container in the freezer for at least 45 minutes to serve in scoops.

Notes

It is best to make this creamy gelato with an ice-cream machine.

Home-made gelato usually benefits from a rest in the freezer for about an hour before serving if you have just made it. Or if it's been in the freezer overnight or even longer, take it out of the freezer about 15 minutes before serving.

Gelato *di* riso

RICE GELATO

There is a well-known Florentine gelateria that is particularly famous for its rice gelato, but it's a flavour that you will find in all good artisan *gelaterie* in Florence these days. It's basically a rice pudding, whipped and frozen, so what you have is a smooth, silky gelato with delightful little frozen pieces of rice.

Makes about 1 litre (34 fl oz/4 cups) of gelato (6–8 serves)

80 g (2¾ oz) short-grain risotto rice, such as arborio or carnaroli

500 ml (17 fl oz/2 cups) full-cream (whole) milk, chilled

½ vanilla bean, split lengthways and seeds scraped

pinch of salt

2 egg yolks

100 g (3½ oz) sugar

200 ml (7 fl oz) milk, warmed

zest of 1 orange

125 ml (4 fl oz/½ cup) pouring (single/light) cream, well chilled

Soak the rice for 30 minutes in cold water and drain. Place the rice in a saucepan with the cold milk, vanilla seeds and salt and cook over a low heat until the rice is very, very soft and the mixture becomes creamy. This should take about 30 minutes. Keep an eye on it, stir occasionally and be careful that the bottom does not burn. Transfer the rice to a bowl to cool.

Prepare a crema (a pouring custard) by whisking the egg yolks with the sugar in a heatproof bowl until very pale and creamy. Add the warm milk, bit by bit, stirring with a wooden spoon until combined. Place the bowl over a bain-marie (double boiler; see page 10) and cook gently over a medium heat, stirring continuously for 10 minutes, or until the eggs reach and stay at 70°C (160°F) for a few minutes. If you don't have a sugar thermometer to check the temperature, it should take about 10 minutes in total and the mixture should thicken ever so slightly and be hot, but not boiling. Draw your finger across the back of the spoon – the line should keep its shape for a few moments. Remove from the heat and stir the rice through the crema along with the orange zest. Chill the mixture thoroughly in the fridge.

Whip the chilled cream until soft peaks form, and gently fold through the chilled rice mixture until combined. Chill in the fridge for 30 minutes, then place in an ice-cream machine and churn according to the manufacturer's instructions until frozen and creamy (see notes). Serve immediately for a softer gelato or put the mixture in an airtight container in the freezer for at least 45 minutes to serve in scoops.

If you have stored the gelato in the freezer overnight or longer, let it stand for 15–20 minutes at room temperature to soften slightly before serving.

Notes

To make this without an ice-cream machine, put the mixture in a sturdy, airtight 1 litre (34 fl oz) container with a fitted lid and freeze for about 5 hours. After about 4 hours, fluff the gelato with a fork. As it loosens, you can begin to beat it with the fork or spoon until the mixture is smooth and rather creamy. Return to the freezer for another hour or so. Fluff again to obtain a creamy and consistent texture before serving. If necessary, let it stand for 15–30 minutes to soften slightly before 'fluffing', beating to soften and serving in soft scoops.

If making the gelato without an ice-cream machine, it is recommended to serve on the day it is made, as it will be creamier. If you want to make it ahead of time and still have that creamy gelato texture, an ice-cream machine is highly recommended.

Sorbetto
di susine

PLUM SORBET

Sorbetto, or sorbet, is one of my favourite ways to preserve ripe, seasonal fruit, and I find stone fruit, including apricots and white peaches, work particularly well in home-made *sorbetto*. But it's the bright colour of damson or blood plums that I really love here, and the beauty of this recipe is that is it so low maintenance – throw the plums in the pot, skins, pits and all. Strain them later.

Makes about 500 ml (17 fl oz/2 cups) of sorbet (about 4 serves)

500 g (1 lb) whole, ripe dark plums, such as damson or blood plums
100 g (3½ oz) sugar
juice of ½ large lemon

Note

Without an ice-cream machine, pour the mixture into a sturdy, shallow container with an airtight lid and place in the freezer for about 5 hours. When frozen, use a fork or spoon to loosen and 'fluff' the sorbet. As it loosens, you can begin to beat it with the fork or spoon until the mixture is smooth and rather creamy. Place back in the freezer and freeze for a further hour. If frozen overnight or longer, it will have hardened and will need to be left at room temperature for 15–20 minutes to soften slightly before 'fluffing', then beating to soften and serving in soft scoops. While this is achievable without an ice-cream machine, the results will be somewhat less creamy on the palate.

Rinse the plums and, without drying them, put them whole in a saucepan over a low–medium heat with 60 ml (2 fl oz/¼ cup) water, covered, and bring to a simmer. As they heat, the plums will release their juices. Check regularly and stir occasionally to make sure they do not stick to the bottom and burn. As they get soft, break them up a little with your wooden spoon. Once simmering, uncover, lower the heat and cook until the plums have released all their juices and have essentially 'melted' down, softening completely, about 10–15 minutes, depending on their size. Remove from the heat and strain the mixture over a bowl (discard the pits) with a food mill or simply with the use of a spatula and a fine-mesh sieve. Set aside to cool.

Place the sugar in a small saucepan with 125 ml (4 fl oz/½ cup) water. Bring to the boil to dissolve the sugar. As soon as it begins to boil, remove from the heat. Let cool slightly then add to the strained plums along with the lemon juice. Let the mixture chill completely before churning in an ice-cream machine according to the manufacturer's instructions (see note). Serve immediately for a soft sorbet or put the mixture in an airtight container in the freezer for about an hour longer to serve in scoops.

Granita *al* melone

MELON GRANITA

Granita is so unbelievably simple to make at home – you don't need any special equipment and it literally takes a few minutes to prepare (waiting hours until you can try it is the only tricky part). This refreshing granita, something between a sorbet and a slushie, is one of my family's favourite ways to enjoy *melone*, much loved especially during the scorching Tuscan summers. It's also surprisingly wonderful with a hint of chilli, which you only sense a few moments after each mouthful – a version I first experienced at a restaurant on Tuscany's Elba Island. Add a touch of dried chilli powder to the mixture before freezing.

Serves 6

150 g (5½ oz) sugar
500–600 g (1 lb 2 oz–1 lb 5 oz) rockmelon (cantaloupe), rind and seeds removed
juice of 1 lemon

Dissolve the sugar in about 125 ml (4 fl oz/½ cup) water in a small saucepan over a low–medium heat and bring to the boil for a few minutes. Remove from the heat and set aside to cool completely.

Chop the melon roughly into pieces. Pulse in a blender or pass through a food mill and reduce to a smooth pulp. Pour the melon pulp into a container that will fit in the freezer (preferably one that has a lid; see note) and stir through the lemon juice and cooled sugar syrup. If the dish doesn't have a lid, double wrap well in plastic wrap. Put the container flat in the freezer and allow 4–6 hours or so to set. Stir every hour with a fork, particularly around the edges where it will freeze first, until you have a creamy but icy consistency. Serve in little glasses with a spoon or straw.

Notes

Choose your container well. You might be left with little choice depending on the shape of your freezer, but consider that if you have the mixture in a wide, shallow dish, such as a glass or ceramic lasagne tray or similar, it will freeze quicker than if you have it in a deep, narrow dish, such as a loaf tin.

If you've left the granita too long (such as overnight) and end up with quite a solid block, simply use a fork to 'fluff' and grate the granita into icy flakes, place into glasses and give it a little stir before serving. You can also make a strawberry or cherry version by substituting the fruit.

Index

About the author

Born in Australia to a Japanese mother and a diplomat Australian father, Emiko Davies has spent most of her life living abroad – her adolescence was spent in China, she attended university in the United States and now, for more than a decade, she has called Italy home.

She first fell in love with Florence as a twenty-year-old art student. She couldn't get the city out of her head and a few years later she returned to study art restoration and photography and soak in the Florentine lifestyle (learning Italian along the way).

Emiko has previously authored three cookbooks; *Florentine* and *Acquacotta* each focus on the traditional, regional dishes of beloved Tuscan places (Florence and the Maremma, respectively), while *Tortellini at Midnight* is a collection of heirloom Italian family recipes from Taranto to Turin to Tuscany.

Emiko continues to write about food and travel within Italy on her blog, as well as for publications such as *Corriere della Sera*, *Gourmet Traveller* and *Conde Nast Traveller*.

She lives in Florence with her Tuscan husband, Marco, and their two young daughters. Wherever she is, the kitchen is the life and heart of her home and where Emiko gathers and cooks with her family each day.

Published in 2021 by Hardie Grant Books, an imprint of Hardie Grant Publishing

Hardie Grant Books (Melbourne)
Building 1, 658 Church Street
Richmond, Victoria 3121

Hardie Grant Books (London)
5th & 6th Floors
52–54 Southwark Street
London SE1 1UN

hardiegrantbooks.com

A catalogue record for this
book is available from the
National Library of Australia

Torta della Nonna
ISBN 978 1 74379 684 9

10 9 8 7 6 5 4 3 2 1

Publishing Director: Jane Willson
Project Editor: Loran McDougall
Design Manager: Mietta Yans
Designer: Studio Polka
Photographers: Lauren Bamford and Emiko Davies
Stylist: Deb Kaloper
Production Manager: Todd Rechner

Colour reproduction by Splitting Image Colour Studio
Printed by Leo Paper Products LTD.

Hardie Grant acknowledges the Traditional Owners of the country on which we
work, the Wurundjeri people of the Kulin nation and the Gadigal people of the
Eora nation, and recognises their continuing connection to the land, waters and
culture. We pay our respects to their Elders past, present and emerging.